Being
BIGGER, BADDER,
BOLDER, BETTER

3-Acts to Redesign Your Blueprint & Rewrite Your Life's Script

Terrah Bennett Smith

D'Lila Publishing
A Legacy Left Behind.

Edited by:
Remington Bennett

Cover Concept - Alicia Shannon

PRINTED IN THE UNITED STATES OF AMERICA

First Printing, 2025
ISBN 979-8-218-68998-8

D'Lila Publishing

Permission can be obtained from terrah.reclaimhaven@gmail.com

is the property of Terrah Bennett Smith

Disclaimer

The information presented in this book is for informational and educational purposes only and does not guarantee success, wealth, or personal growth. The author, publisher, and affiliates assume no responsibility for any loss—mental, physical, emotional, financial, or otherwise—arising from the use or application of the content provided herein.

This book is intended as a guide and should be treated as such. Results may vary, and any actions taken based on the content are at the reader's own risk. The author, publisher, and affiliates make no warranties or representations regarding the accuracy, applicability, or effectiveness of the content.

If you are experiencing mental, physical, or emotional difficulties, we strongly recommend seeking appropriate professional help. The author, publisher, and affiliates expressly disclaim any liability for any consequences resulting from the use of this book.

It's 2012, and I've decided to write a book about my journey.
It's 2013, and I've decided to sit down and finish this book.
It's 2015, and… yup, still working on finishing that book.
It's 2016, and I've started again… and then
put the book down because, well, life.
It's 2017, and once again, I've decided to finish my
book about my journey (fingers crossed this time!).
It's 2018, and… okay, I really want to finish
this book about my journey. But life. Again.
It's 2019, and… you know what? Forget the book. Who needs it?
It's 2020, and I've decided: No, really, I want to finish my book
about my journey. It'll happen this year. For sure.
It's 2022, and I'm trying to finish my book about my journey.
Emphasis on "trying."
It's 2024, and I've decided—no more excuses—I will
finally finish my book about my journey.
It's May 2024, AND I HAVE SAT DOWN TO FINALLY
COMPLETE MY BOOK… AND IT'S DONE!

AHHHH, NO IT'S NOT! –

It's January 2025, and my new goal is to release it and kick
things off with my first "Being Bigger, Badder, Bolder, Better"
workshop on my birthday, June 29th.

WISH ME LUCK! Or, better yet, send dessert and wine. 🍷🍰

I could feel bad for all the missed deadlines. But why?

Remembering to adjust, and realign with your desired journey, is all part of the Journey.

It's a process. No need to beat yourself up for missed deadlines, or unachieved goals. Simply realign with what came through you to do, and set new goals.

Remember, if it came through you,

it's for YOU to do!

Reader Discretion Advised

This book contains references to emotional and mild physical abuse. If you find yourself triggered in any way while reading or reflecting on your own experiences, please take care of yourself and seek support. It's important to acknowledge your emotions and reach out for help when needed.

Below are a few helplines that can offer assistance:

National Suicide Prevention Lifeline:
Call 988 (or 800-273-8255) - 24/7

SAMHSA (Substance Abuse and Mental Health Services Administration):
Call 800-662-4357

Crisis Text Line:
Text "HOME" to 741741

Please note: This book is not a substitute for professional therapy or counseling. If you are in need of professional support, please seek guidance from a licensed therapist or counselor.

There is nothing wrong with asking for help.

Dedication

To my mother, **Dorothy Lila Smith (Maybank)**, a beautiful woman who, on August 24, 1974, made her transition shortly after her firstborn daughter's high school graduation. I write this book as an homage to you. It's been almost 50 years, and not a day goes by that I am not reminded of you.

When I look at one of my son's gorgeous, chiseled cheekbones, my other son's big, rounded eyes, and—most of all—my daughter's kindness, graciousness, and loyalty to me, her mom… there you are. Then there are the songs of the 1960s, especially one of my favorites, *Sweet Caroline*, which instantly paints a vivid picture in my mind—of you singing and attempting your version of the popular dance at that time.

I owe you my ability to persevere. You indirectly taught me how to turn wine into water. Your creativity and desire to give to others in need, even when we, your family, were in need, was honorable. Your role as a mother—both to us and to others—has left a lasting impact, one that has been replicated by myself and many others fortunate enough to have crossed your path.

I dedicate this book to the loves of my life—my three children. I could not have designed you any better. Your ability to listen and take heed of advice, your level of respect, and your passion for growth fill me with joy as I watch you navigate your journeys. You are a force. You've mastered the art of staying on a high vibration and recognize the importance of learning from each experience. As a result, you've been able to design your own blueprints and, in turn, create the life you desire to live.

My last dedication is to *me*.

I appreciate you for doing the frickin' work. I appreciate you for choosing to work on yourself before deciding to bring children into this world. I appreciate you for making the choice to teach them from the best of what you have learned—and for being honest enough with yourself to share where you went wrong and self-correct.

And to you, my readers—thank you for choosing me today.

LEARN. BE EMPOWERED. ENJOY!

TABLE OF CONTENTS

HEY Y'ALL

Being Bigger, Badder, Bolder, Better (5B's) is a short and sweet read covering various aspects of my life. I'll share what I've learned and how I've connected the dots of my journey so I could see what needed to change—specifically, the things that weren't aligned with a high vibration.

You might find some repetitive verbiage. Hopefully, you'll notice that this repetition occurs because our varying habits are born from the same core. They're disguised with different faces, names, and situations—but the core is the same. Therefore, the language needed to reprogram them will sound familiar.

I'm not a doctor, and I haven't obtained a degree in what I'm about to share with you. There are people who've gone to school, earned degrees, and studied how the brain and human behavior work. They use their credentials to serve others in need. I've been blessed in many ways; however, academic study has never been a passion of mine—unless the book taught me something that could propel my spiritual growth forward. If it didn't make logical sense to me, I wasn't (and still am not) interested, and I move on.

Since 1987, however, I began studying to self-correct. I started my journey to acquire my "Life Certification." I spent countless hours—years, actually—listening, studying, and attending seminars and workshops to learn how to apply this work to my life. I put together my own program, which I fine-tuned and used on myself to create change. Over the years, I've shared it with friends and used it as the foundation for several workshops. Many have been blessed by the results.

Now, I'm sharing my workshop—in short-book form—with you. The choice is yours: either take this ride with me, or, if you prefer to gain knowledge from a licensed doctor or therapist, please return this sweet little book and get your money back.

This book is not intended to be a comprehensive guide with all the answers for your personal journey. I crafted it for myself, and it proved to be a powerful, life-changing resource. So, I decided to share what I've learned with you, in hopes that as you read, you'll recognize the connections between my story, the events that shaped my life, and how I found clarity by taking responsibility for my thoughts and actions.

I use my story as a mirror for you to reflect upon, because so often, we can see ourselves in others and their stories. Hopefully, you'll discern where the dots have connected—or where they still need to be—as you continue along your path.

My hope is that it resonates with you in a way that encourages reflection on your past steps, helping you see how they've affected your current path.

I want you to look back on your life and pay attention to each piece— each person, food habit, moment of happiness, sadness, favorite outfit, and as many little details as you can. This doesn't mean revisiting painful experiences. Our focus should remain on the outcomes we want to manifest and the high-vibrational energy that will help us get there.

I've allotted space for you to journal along the way, but if you have a lot to write, you might want to keep your own "5B's" journal handy. This will be helpful as we move forward. You'll find yourself having many "Aha!" moments—times you'll want to jot down thoughts, track patterns, and notice when *you* (or certain people) show up as the common denominator. As you move through the chapters, I hope you'll begin to see how certain habits were formed early on, and feel excited about the journey to correct them.

Remember: it's never too late to change. As long as you have breath, you have another opportunity to live the life you desire.

*"I am not what happened to me, I am what
I choose to become"*

Carl Jung

* * *

"You alone are responsible for your life.
It doesn't matter what your mama said or did,
or what your daddy did or said—or the bully who
taunted you in the sixth grade.
You are the responsible party for how you're choosing to
allow those experiences to affect your life now.
It's time to make a change. So pay attention to the
energy you create, because when it goes out,
you will be the reason for what returns.
You cannot sow lemons and reap sweet apples."

Terrah Bennett Smith

* * *

FOREWARD

From Debra to Terrah

The rule of thumb when writing a book is that the foreword is usually written by someone other than the author. Well, as I've mentioned, I don't always follow what is said or taught—unless it makes sense to me. So, the foreword in this book could very well be written by me.

Why?

Because I have grown to know there's more than just one person living in my head. There's the grown-up woman, whom most people know as Terrah Bennett Smith, and the other me, known to my very close friends and family as Debra.

This foreword is written by Debra on behalf of Terrah.

I have had the pleasure of watching Terrah grow into a fine young woman—from a closet-insecure little girl who knew how to mask her feelings to a confident, empowered woman who is no longer afraid to speak her truth. I am honored to write this foreword because when you see someone put in the level of work it takes to enhance their life, it should be celebrated however they feel best—reflecting them and their journey.

When you get to the place of such inner peace that you can share your story without concern for judgment, you've arrived. Terrah is spreading her wings and *finally* taking flight.

I have watched her many times not owning her greatness, and I would get so frustrated watching her live in the past—with me. My inability to move forward kept her stagnant, standing just a foot away from the spotlight. I can't tell you how many times I, and others, have shown up on her behalf and tried to nudge her. Depending on the person, the nudge ranged from ever so slight to literally kicking her butt straight into the light.

I'd watch her struggle with periodic moments of enjoying her success, only to self-sabotage and retreat back to her place of comfort. I'm sure many of you can relate. Even still, she had a resilience unlike most. Her ability to pick herself up and start again… and again… and again, was unmatched.

Eventually, she became so frustrated with her own repetitive patterns that her desire to honor her greatness became stronger than the pull of her never-ending rollercoaster of pain.

The moment she began to let go of things and people who didn't lift her up energetically was the moment it became clear—she was ready to live in her light. In her truth.

She began to lovingly speak her truth about herself—to herself and to others—no longer feeling embarrassed when sharing her goals. After all, she realized:

"What you think of me is none of my business."

Although moments of fear would still rear their ugly head, they no longer stole focus as they had done so often in the past. The process was magnificent to witness.

Terrah took over. She took charge. That's when she could finally get some rest.

Debra, the little girl stuck in time, got to step aside and allow Terrah to soar. Thank you.

The other wonderful part is that Terrah has never asked me, Debra, to leave or not be a part of her continued journey. She welcomes me, and still allows old friends to refer to me as Debra. That name has—and will always be—reserved for the important people from an important time in her life.

She's made it clear that without me, there would have been no need for the journey.

INTRODUCTION
Why?

A "friend" once asked me, "Terrah, how does it feel to watch so many people you know 'make it,' while you have not succeeded in the entertainment industry?"

I remember feeling like a knife had been stuck in my chest. Why would someone ask me such a thing? It was quite insulting. At first, I wanted to lash out and give her a few choice words. But instead, I took a deep breath and remembered my own words: when you point a finger at someone, three point back at you. Meaning, people come into your life to show you who you are.

So, I calmed myself before responding. "Let's see," I said. "I have done everything I wanted on a professional level. I've performed on Broadway, I was a Top 40 recording artist, I've starred in, directed, and written for television, stage, and screen. I have mentored and inspired many, raised three amazing children, and now I've written my first book."

I looked at her and said, "I'm GOOD."

I've often had the thought that I've done so much, and still, no one knows who I am—which, of course, isn't actually true. My friend's statement was a reflection of my inner belief. Once I took the idea of what my success was supposed to look like out of my head and started living in the enjoyment of my accomplishments, my life began to change… FOR REAL! I realized my focus was on the wrong things—how YOU, THEY, THEM, Y'ALL view me. And I gave value to everything that went along with that. Not all the time, but enough for it to subconsciously affect my life.

Now, that may not be your situation—but you're reading this book. Why? Hmm, let me guess. Is it that you want to change some things in your life, and you're curious how this average Joe-sephine (me) went from rags to riches? Well, that's what I'm sharing with you. I was able to do it, and this book will show you how I got there.

"Remember, riches come in many forms, not just money—so don't sleep on it!"

Why did I write it? Why should you read it? Why do I believe you will benefit from it?

To start, the self-improvement industry is estimated to be worth $11 billion in the United States alone. Why? Perhaps because so many of us are in search of more—both inside and out. And I gather, since you've gotten this far into the book, you too are in search of change.

Why did things finally change for me?

After many years of being one of those millions of people on the quest for self-improvement, I asked myself: Why am I continually circling the abyss of my own stuckness? WHY? No matter how many books I read, seminars I attended, vision boards I created, tapes I listened to, or videos I watched, I would eventually find myself right back in the same spot.

There was a time I felt nothing good would come my way because I was born into a family that was jinxed. We had moments of wins, but for the most part, they were fleeting. This rollercoaster went on for years, and the more it repeated, the more I cemented the idea that I was doomed to live out the cards I had been dealt.

It wasn't until I got sick and tired of being sick and tired that I became determined to find a solution. I started by paying close attention and looking for the similarities between those I believed were able to manifest the things in their lives I was working hard to acquire. What did they have in common?

One of the main things that stuck out was their wiring. What was at the core of their beliefs? Even though I thought I had it all going on, my core belief was a fear of being grand. I played myself small and expected to be rewarded with great things.

Thus began the process of reprogramming.

It wasn't easy, because I had cemented patterns that came with much more than a quick vision board fix. I created and followed my own program and found the results to be quite phenomenal. This is why you're here, and I look forward to sharing what I did with you.

> *"The key is understanding that cemented patterns don't disappear*
> *—you can acquire tools to stay ahead of them and know*
> *how to handle them when they resurface."*

WORDS/PHRASES TO FAMILIARIZE YOURSELF WITH

Vortex – A concept I learned from Abraham/Esther Hicks. Think of the vortex as a special place where all your desires are kept, waiting for you to be ready for them. To get into the vortex, you need to focus on things that make you happy and avoid things that hold you back.

Contrast – This is when you come across something you don't like. In life, you'll always find things you wish were different or better. Whether you complain about them or simply wish for change, it shows you want to grow and improve naturally.

High Vibration – These are feelings of joy, appreciation, freedom, love, and empowerment. They lift you up and help you stay connected to the best version of yourself.

Low Vibration – These are feelings like fear, despair, desperation, grief, and powerlessness. They bring you down and make it harder to feel good.

Rowing Upstream – Another concept from Abraham/Esther Hicks. Just like in a real stream, nobody wants to paddle against the current. It takes too much effort, feels exhausting, and isn't much fun.

Rowing Downstream – The opposite of rowing upstream. When you're in the flow of positive thoughts, it's like paddling downstream. Things come more easily, and life feels easier and more enjoyable.

Alignment – This is when you feel truly happy and connected to something bigger than yourself. It's about being at peace with what's happening and feeling good inside. Instead of just going through the motions, it's about feeling good in your heart. When your thoughts, feelings, and actions align with what makes you happy, life becomes more satisfying. It's about focusing on things that make you feel good, picking thoughts that uplift you, and doing things that excite you about your goals.

Pain Body – A term I learned from Eckhart Tolle, which refers to the "energy field of old but still very much alive emotion that lives in almost every human being." It's the emotional baggage we carry with us, affecting our present thoughts and feelings.

We all live our lives in acts. Act One, our childhood, is when our blueprint is designed, and the seeds are planted. Whether aware of it or not, we all are blindly planting seeds (beliefs) on a daily basis. Most of the time, we are oblivious and believe we are just doing, saying, or being a certain way, and that it does not have an effect on us. But the power behind the words we choose to speak or the thoughts we think are not weightless. They carry energy.

***

Scene #1

LIVING IN THE LAP OF LUXURY... ~~NOT...~~ YET!

It was a beautiful summer day in June. The sun shone brightly as random neighborhood kids zoomed by on their bicycles and roller skates, sneaking glimpses at the neighborhood newcomers. All the families moving in at this time were first-time dwellers. Beefy movers bustled about, lugging furniture from various moving trucks into the building. The trucks were scheduled carefully, allowing each family to complete their move during their allotted time. It was now the Banks family's turn to unload their belongings.

An excited Dee hopped out of her father's car and gazed up at the brand-new high-rise building.

"It's tall. What floor do we live on?" she asked.

"Fourteenth," her father replied.

Lee and Dot were Dee's parents. They had three children, and Dee was smack dab in the middle. Yep, a middle child. Some say middle children come with their own set of challenges.

As they made their way into the building, Dee examined the lobby and whispered to her sister, "Wow, they have milk machines."

"Woohoo, we've arrived!"

You couldn't tell Dee they weren't living in the lap of luxury. They were rich!

At that time, Dee had no idea what the term "projects" meant—but she would find out soon enough. It became clear when the Webster Projects apartment building quickly went from luxurious to "ghetto fabulous." The milk machines gave way to the milkman delivering orders to your door, which eventually gave way to, "You better get your butt to the store and buy a quart of milk."

Dee had a vivid imagination. She spent much of her childhood flipping through magazines of beautiful homes, fantasizing about the day she'd have one of her own. While many of the neighborhood kids adapted to life in the "projects," Dee held on to that fleeting sense of luxury she felt when she first entered the lobby.

The Webster Projects, like most neighborhoods in the Bronx, were alive with vibrant, nightly energy. Most weekends, as the sun began to set, Webster Avenue came alive with the sound of congas, bongos, shakers, and other percussion instruments. The Puerto Rican brothers and sisters brought so much life to this inner-city neighborhood with their impromptu jam sessions.

Unfortunately for Dee, her curfew was strictly enforced at the dimming of the streetlights. Most of her fun had to be enjoyed from her 14th-floor kitchen window. The sounds of salsa music, the language, and the rhythmic banging and bonging of congas floated up the building and into her home. This was the balcony seat for her personal viewing pleasure.

Memories of those late-night jam sessions, park sprinklers, illegally spewing fire hydrants, 14th-floor talent shows, extra salty pumpkin seeds, Lemonhead candies, and WABC radio made the madness in Dee's life more bearable. Still, some painful memories stayed etched in the forefront of her mind.

Unbeknownst to Dee, growing up in the "inner city" was a stepping stone to a larger and more promising life. At the time, she had no idea that her mother's strict boundaries would benefit her in the long run. Unable to roam the streets or stay outside after the streetlights came on, Dee redirected her boredom into daydreaming and fantasizing.

Her favorite fantasy involved walking through a big house of her own and sipping tea in her backyard. This vision had such a positive impact on her that it made it difficult for Dee to live in anything less than what she imagined—and she never did.

Meanwhile, her less-than-positive fantasies also surfaced, but in a less desirable way.

"Pinch the nose, hold the head back, and make sure to arch the neck to keep blood from running down her face," was one of them.

She dreaded it. "Stop! Stop!" Dee would cry.

She was very young when these incidents began, and though she only recalled it happening once or twice, the impression was long-lasting. Dee suffered from severe allergies, and chronic nosebleeds were a part of it. In an attempt to stop the bleeding, her parents would lay her on the kitchen counter with her face under the running faucet. Who knows if this was a legitimate cure or just an old-fashioned, passed-down remedy, but it scared the life out of Dee and became another cemented block in her foundation of fears.

FANTASIES TO REALITIES

Apartment 14B was where the Banks family called home for eleven years. This three-bedroom, one-bath apartment became the birthplace of Dee's aspirations for stardom. The parents on this floor—mothers in particular—were known to be stricter than others in the building. They had an unspoken bond: if one of them witnessed one of their children doing something out of line, you could count on your mother hearing about it before you even heard her key in the door, and consequences would follow. Dee and her friends had their own code: Mum's the word.

In the middle of each floor in this twenty-one-story building was an enclosed terrace with a concrete bench for seating and a wrought-iron fence with diamond-shaped openings. This gave the kids visibility to the world outside while keeping them safe. Dee loved spending hours on the community terrace, playing with her friends, but most importantly, putting on talent shows. She was a budding actress, singer, and dancer, as well as a natural entrepreneur. She ran the whole show, selecting the songs, choosing the clothing, and deciding who sang what.

Dee made her family and friends buy tickets to sit on the cold bench and watch the performances, which they obliged with mild reluctance. Although Dee was talented enough to be considered the "Diana Ross" of the Supremes in her productions, she was content being just one of the ensemble members. She convinced herself she didn't care much about being in the spotlight—it was all just for fun—but secretly, she dreamt of something bigger: becoming a "TV star."

Outside of one friend on the 14th floor, no one else in her neighborhood knew about Dee's goal of being on television. She was embarrassed by it, fearing that sharing her dream would make her an outcast. To fit in, she played herself small, doing just enough to blend with her peers. And guess what? For years, life returned to her "just enough." Though Dee achieved some success, it was just enough to avoid standing out.

Still, you can't hide from your truth. While she appeared comfortable as part of life's ensemble, Dee had an innate knack for doing a little something extra that brought attention to her special talents. Even so, she continued to live within the confines of her small inner cubicle.

The one thing Dee knew for sure was that she loved performing. Anything else felt like a challenge when it came to focusing. School, long church sermons, and stories that didn't interest her were frustrating to sit through. She resonated only with things that fed her spirit and wanted to quickly move on from anything that didn't. Dee was often labeled hyperactive and told she needed to sit still. Today, she might have been diagnosed with ADHD and put on medication.

Dee had a vivid imagination, with ideas flowing constantly. She wondered why it was so easy for her to move from one thought to another, create one idea after another, and flip between them with ease. At one point, she was convinced something was wrong with her. It took years for her to realize this was a gift—her superpower.

Dee's inability to sit idle motivated her to organize talent shows. She hated waiting for others to make things happen, which propelled her to take the initiative. She was a naturally born leader, but when asked if she aspired to become a director, she scoffed at the idea.

As Dee continued hiding in her shadow, her behavior birthed a less confident young woman. She grew increasingly frustrated watching others live their dreams to the fullest.

"Why do they get to have what they want in life and not me?" Dee often wondered if she was being punished. Raised in a church that equated blessings with behavior, Dee tried to be as nice and thoughtful as possible.

Guess what? Nothing changed. She could only surmise that she just wasn't good enough.

So began her descent into the land of "not-enough-isms." What other explanation could there be? "I'm just as talented as they are," she'd say. But did she really believe it? Years of growing up without enough food, money, and self-confidence buried themselves deep within her and were now resurfacing. No amount of praying, tithing extra money, or being the best girl ever seemed to change things, and Dee tried them all. She believed something external was keeping her from the life she desired, and she was determined to figure it out. She never realized the change had to come from within.

Years of watching others live the life she wanted became harder to bear. Dee resorted to pretending she had it all. On the outside, she appeared grand. "Fake it 'til you make it" became her mantra. She walked with her head held high, looking like a million dollars but often having only fifty cents in her bank account—and even less in her pocket. Dee never let her outer shell show her inner turmoil. She refused to appear broken or poor to anyone.

Oddly enough, her faking it helped her stay in alignment with her higher self. Though she didn't feel empowered, the message she sent out was: "I'm a badass, and you will see that." That's how most people perceived her.

Unfortunately, Dee's subconscious vibrated more with her cemented belief in "not-enough-isms." If only she could shift her focus and align with the greatness awaiting her. She would see how her reluctance to take leadership roles or audition for lead characters stemmed from her lack of confidence. She would also recognize how much she valued outsiders' approval—and how unworthy she felt when she didn't receive it. For years, fear kept her blinded, comfortable, and living in a pretend fantasy world.

Can you recall a time when, despite your circumstances, you indulged in fantasies about what your life could be? That moment when you believed you could turn your dreams into reality before the naysayers—or your inner doubts—crept in?

I bet you can vividly remember at least one of those fantasies. Dig deep; they're still there, tucked away. As you recall them, notice how your energy shifts and perhaps even brings a smile to your face.

I challenge you to pause here and close your eyes. Put on some feel-good music that reminds you of your childhood. Focus on the dreams you had—the ones that made you feel warm and fuzzy inside—and write them down. Only the dreams, and how they made you feel. In the next exercise, we'll dive into the dreams that never manifested or were buried away, and work on replacing and reprogramming them.

Exercise #1 - DREAM BIG

> **PLEASE WRITE YOUR UNINHIBITED FANTASY/DREAM – NO MATTER HOW UNREALISTIC, WRITE AS MUCH ABOUT IT AS YOU CAN REMEMBER. IT'S VERY IMPORTANT TO INCLUDE AS MUCH DETAILS AS POSSIBLE.**

(Example) I remember when I was three years old, I used to dream of being a ballerina. I went to see a dance show with my mom, and the girls were so beautiful I wanted to dance. That was when I set out to be a ballerina, and I would dance all day long in my bedroom. I'd watch every movie that had dancers in it. I was determined I could do it..

Time to take a trip down fantasy lane. Write down as many fantasies, daydreams, hopes and wishes you remember. While doing it try to remember and feel the emotion that accompanied it.

_____

_____

_____

_____

_____

_____

_____

_____

_____

_____

_____

Scene #2

ROUND ONE – *Ding - Ding!*

Let the Games Begin

"Faking it…" did not shield Dee from dealing with life's contrasts. They were ever-present and relentless. It seemed that once she gave energy to one "upstream contrasting energetic situation," other upstream situations inevitably followed. Dee was addicted to certain behaviors—rooted and cemented in her psyche. It was strange how uncomfortably comfortable she felt with them. Life without these habits felt empty.

Dee realized that the hardest part of change was remembering not to repeat the same choices she'd made before. She was operating on autopilot; her addictions had morphed into ingrained behaviors. The only way to regain control over her reactions was to get ahead of these behaviors, but at that point, she had no idea what that meant. Even if she did, she had no clue how to accomplish it.

Let's dig deeper into Dee's cemented "not-enough-isms."

Sticks and Stones

You remember the old saying: "Sticks and stones may break my bones, but words will never harm me." If only Dee truly believed those words. In reality, she felt every stick and stone thrown at her, and the pain caused by those words stayed with her for years.

Dee had plenty of "stick and stone" nicknames. "Chester" was a name given to her by a few neighborhood boys because of her overdeveloped breasts—36C, to be exact. That might not sound so bad, but at fourteen years old, Dee was tall and lanky. More often than not, people saw her breasts coming down the street before they saw her. Then there was "Big Nose," another infamous nickname, and to Dee, it was the worst of all.

Most of Dee's teenage years were spent in embarrassment—over one thing or another. On top of growing up in a household with minimal income and food, she wrestled with inner turmoil about her looks, her habit of playing small, and her fear of anyone she knew discovering her talents. While Dee could confidently sing on stage in front of strangers and shine, the moment she noticed someone she knew in the audience or heard they'd listened to her music, she cringed with embarrassment. She lived in a constant state of self-judgment, subconsciously projecting that judgment outward.

Growing up in a household with a sister the neighborhood kids dubbed "the pretty sister" only compounded Dee's insecurities. It wasn't just the kids in the neighborhood who made these comparisons; strangers did it, too. Dee vividly remembers riding the train with her sister when two guys sitting across from them commented about them being sisters. One said, "Yeah, but she's the pretty one," clearly pointing to Dee's sister.

Though Dee had grown numb to such remarks, they still stung. She let them roll off her back—or so she thought. These dialogues, while familiar, were not something she wanted to hear or be reminded of repeatedly.

All those years of Dee soldering habits into behaviors eventually had to manifest into something. And they did—it was called Dee's journey.

Dee began to see all her fantasies, daydreams, and negative thoughts bear fruit. The emotions and beliefs from her past were so deeply ingrained that it was difficult for her to recognize them as non-truths—ideas that could be challenged and changed.

Contrast

+

Focus

=

Change

* * *

SAYING OVER AND OVER THAT YOU'RE GOING TO CHANGE A BAD HABIT

=

CONTINUES TO BRING FOCUS TO THAT HABIT

=

KEEPING THAT HABIT ALIVE AND ACTIVE

A professor of social psychology at Florida State University, Roy F. Baumeister, co-authored a journal article in The Review of General Psychology titled "Bad Is Stronger Than Good." In the article, Baumeister stated, "Research shows this is a basic and wide-ranging principle of psychology." He elaborated: "Bad emotions, bad parents, and bad feedback have more impact than good ones. Bad impressions and bad stereotypes are quicker to form and more resistant to disconfirmation than good ones."

It's fascinating how the brain works—especially when it has experienced trauma. Somewhere in Dee's mind, there were likely plenty of warm and fuzzy memories from her childhood. Yet because the pain of unpleasant memories carried more weight, when she thought about her parents' relationship, the financial struggles, and other challenges, the sweet moments faded into the background.

Take Dee's nosebleeds, for example. Even in situations where the intentions were good, if something didn't feel good to her, her young mind had a way of transforming it into something negative. That negativity took root and eventually ran amok. It would take years before Dee became aware of the chemical sensations in her body whenever she succumbed to those negative thoughts.

Start today by being grateful for understanding the importance of the energy you emanate and consciously directing that energy toward your desired outcomes. Be thankful that, as of now, you realize change requires being conscious of your unconscious self. You can only attract the good you desire by focusing on things that carry a high vibration and transmit positive energy. Only then will more of the same be returned to you.

Divorcing yourself from someone or a situation doesn't mean you'll automatically divorce the associated habits. Of course, this depends on the individual. Some people have an iron will, refusing to engage in past behaviors and avoiding anything resembling them. Dee, unfortunately, wasn't one of those people.

It's crucial to pay close attention to the words you speak and the energy they carry. What you send out with an energetic charge will return to you. When you plant a lemon tree, you don't expect it to bear apples, do you? Of course not—you'll get lemons. So why expect negative thoughts you send into the universe to yield positive outcomes? And trust that the more energy you invest in those negative thoughts, the more powerful their manifestation will be.

The good news? Energy is always exchangeable. Since we have full control over our energy, we can redirect our thoughts and focus to produce positive outcomes whenever we decide to do so. Dee would need to divorce her old beliefs and align herself with the life she wanted to create. Only then could her brain begin rewiring itself, forming a new neurological framework that allowed her to feel and act like the person she aspired to become.

The path to recovery and rediscovery comes from the work you do on yourself—not your career, not another person, place, or thing. Imagine planting your very own *"I want to fall in love with me"* tree and watching it flourish. Can you envision truly falling in love with yourself?

When you achieve this, seeking external validation becomes unnecessary because you've fulfilled that need from within. We've all heard the phrase, *"You can't love anyone until you love yourself first."* It's a common saying tossed around casually, but few possess the tools to genuinely live by it. Going even deeper and actually *falling in love with yourself* takes this a step further.

By doing so, you eliminate the need for love or validation from external sources. You'll still enjoy the company of others, look forward to spending time with them, and share fun experiences. However, external praise or accolades will no longer penetrate your self-worth in the same way. If someone falls short or retracts their affection, you won't feel deprived, and they won't walk away with pieces of *you*.

Why? Because they were merely the icing on an already delicious cake… you. And as we all know, icing can often be overly sweet and extra fattening.

"Thoughts cause biochemical reactions in your brain that release chemical signals, and those chemical signals make the body feel exactly the way you were just thinking."

Dr. Joe Dispenza

* * *

Your Thoughts
+
Your Energy
=
Your Life

When you acknowledge a painful contrast, avoid dwelling on how much it annoys you or questioning why it appeared. Instead, replace it with a good-feeling thought or action. Take Dee's situation with her boss as an example: he's just arrived in a foul mood, ranting and using her as his verbal punching bag. Not even "faking it" or "being it" could shield Dee from the disruptive energy his tyranny brings. So, what are her options?

She could go toe-to-toe with him or cower and wallow in her feelings. Both choices would keep her vibrating on a lower energetic tier, rowing upstream. Alternatively, she could go inward, focusing on her upcoming vacation in two weeks. She could mentally plan her wardrobe, schedule a hair appointment, or pick out new luggage—all while sitting at her desk, smiling at her boss. This shift in focus creates a *pattern interrupt*, redirecting her energy to a higher tier and allowing her to row downstream.

I love the concepts of rowing upstream and downstream—thank you, Abraham Hicks! We should aim to keep our focus on things that present the least resistance. Figure out what that looks like for you. Depending on the circumstances, it's helpful to have a few go-to options ready to use as needed.

When you spend energy denouncing what you *don't* want to do, your focus remains on that very thing, inadvertently feeding it more energy. Since like-energy attracts like-energy, you'll draw more of what you're trying to avoid. Even when you exert effort *trying* not to think about something, the energy spent in the attempt means you're rowing upstream, and you'll only encounter more resistance. However, when you replace those thoughts with good-feeling ones, you elevate your energy to a higher tier, attracting more positive experiences in return.

Dr. Linda Logan, a friend of Dee's, often told her, "If you want to know what you believe about yourself, look at your life." While Dee knew there was truth in those words, accepting them was a bitter pill to swallow. "Why would I do this to myself?" she wondered. "I would never want to live like this on purpose."

Not *on purpose*, Dee, but you did. Remember all those years of carelessly giving energy to your thoughts and feelings? Those habits became cemented, and voilà—your lemon tree bore lemons. Sometimes, the hardest part of change is identifying what needs to change. Once you've made that decision, you must start chipping away at the old, cemented behavior patterns. It's about reprogramming. Practice makes perfect.

Our brains constantly reference present situations through the lens of past experiences, which hinders us from breaking free of outdated patterns and behaviors. Without a *pattern interrupt*, the brain continues creating neural pathways tied to those past experiences, making behaviors automatic and habitual over time. Writing things down in a workbook can help kick-start change, but let's face it—most of us don't have the time or opportunity to grab a workbook whenever we need to reset.

So, let's take this exercise to the streets and make it fun. We're going to throw a *"PATTERN INTERRUPT"* party!

When feelings become the means of thinking, or if we cannot think greater than how we feel, we can never change.

Joe Dispenza.

* * *

New neural connections are constantly being soldered into place on a multitude of issues. We are bombarded with feelings of "not pretty enough, not thin enough, not tall enough, not smart enough…" Most of us have, or had, at least one *not-enough-ism*. These feelings often arrive with a large set of emotional luggage, planning to stay for a while. If you're lucky, you'll nip them in the bud early, send them on their way, and never look back.

Let's take a closer look at Dee's life and list a few of the cemented neural connections she would later have to chip away at:

- There was her extra-beautiful sister, and the constant reminders of just how beautiful she was.
- There was the lack of food, along with the embarrassment of periodically having to borrow meat from neighbors to complete their meals.
- There was that colorful food stamp money she had to present when grocery shopping.
- There was the government food delivered to their home—although, admittedly, that brick block of cheddar cheese was tasty back then.
- There was the image of her mother sitting and staring out their 14th-floor window with a look of doom on her face. *That* was the worst.

You might say, "This doesn't sound so bad. You should hear what "I" went through as a child." The truth is, if you asked ten friends, nine of them would likely share emotionally challenging childhood stories. It's not a contest for the worst story; it's about how those experiences affected us and the neural connections formed because of them.

Another cemented behavior Dee mastered came later in her teen years. Initially, her pride kept her from asking for what she wanted or needed—she didn't want anyone to see how broken she felt inside. By continuing to share her woe-is-me story, she unknowingly began manipulating people into feeling sorry for her. Telling her tale of hardship made her seem like a hero to some. "Wow! You made it through that? That's amazing!" But even this behavior carried energy—and it wasn't the good kind.

Dee knew nothing about concepts like *the law of attraction* or the idea that *like energy attracts like situations*. She was unaware that her years of fantasizing about physical abuse (because that's what she saw and knew) were creating neural connections and a chemical addiction her mind and body would later crave. It took years for her to recognize the chemical response her body produced whenever these cravings arose.

Eventually, Dee began to notice an uncomfortable, hot, bubbling sensation. It felt like a warning, a harbinger of something bad. Initially, the feeling wasn't tied to anything specific—it was just a sensation. But over time, she observed that it was often followed by a negative event. This sensation became what she called the *"something bad is about to happen"* feeling, and she grew to fear it. What made it worse was that it often appeared right after good news. Dee began equating good news with impending disaster: "No need to get overly excited; the other shoe is going to drop—and it's not a good shoe."

After years of diligent self-work, Dee developed tools to rewire her mind and body. She learned how to replace the chemical cravings of *"something bad is on its way"* with the anticipation of *"something great is about to happen."* It wasn't easy, but she did it—and it changed her life.

Had Dee or her mother understood this concept earlier, they could have spared themselves years of pain. The *how-to* of conditioning and rewiring is something that must be developed over time, but the rewards are transformative.

Situation	Replacement
Borrowing meat from Neighbors	Deciding to be healthy and eat a vegetarian diet even for that night.
Food Stamps, food shopping	How smart my mother was to find a way for us to eat
Limited Christmas Presents	Do a one gift exchange and decide to honor Christmas as a time to give thanks

You get the idea. Any of these replacements would have served as a pattern-interrupt for Dee and a very different and more positive habitual behavior would have formed.

Emotional or physical trauma produces hormones in the body that converge on the brain in such a way that a neural connection is instantly soldered into place which then creates habitual behaviors (blocks) that are difficult to see around without therapeutic assistance

Dr. Linda Logan

* * *

Trauma

+

Neural Connections

=

Habitual Behaviors

Exercise #2 – BEING IT

The power of the pen is mighty. Answering the questions below will help you better understand the person you have become today. If you take the time to reflect and write about moments from your childhood when you thought you were doing something "just for fun," you might notice a surprising connection between those activities and what has actually manifested in your life.

Fantasy	How Often did you attempt?	Still pursuing Y/N	If not why & do you love what you do now?	If given the opportunity would you do it now ?Y/N	What steps could you take to do it now?
Acting	Every weekend	Yes		Y	

Fantasy	How Often did you attempt?	Still pursuing Y/N	If not why & do you love what you do now?	If given the opportunity would you do what your heart desires now Y/N & why?	What steps could you take to do it now?

PATTERN INTERRUPT

For the rest of this week, observe yourself closely. If you catch yourself sharing a negative thought, offering unsolicited opinions, or saying phrases like, "I know, because…"—stop right there. **PATTERN INTERRUPT.**

Instead of saying, "I know, because…," try shifting your perspective. For example, say:

- "I've never spoken to that person, so I really have no idea why they did that or what they meant."

Or if you find yourself thinking, "My sister always told me that I'm not attractive," interrupt that pattern with:

- "I am so grateful for my growth. Words that once hurt me now empower me, aligning me with everything beautiful about myself."

Exercise #3 REPLACEMENT

DATE	STATEMENT	REPLACEMENT
2/1/24	When I look at you Dee, I don't understand why you have not made it yet (I initially took this as something was wrong with me, because I had not made it yer - whatever "made it" is)	I am thrilled that my friend's words catalyzed for me to realize that the external world perceives me on a much larger scale than the smaller version I hold of myself. So, I silently thanked her.
2/1/24	My friend just passed away and I can't seem to move forward with life. I'm feeling broken and lost	I'm so thankful for the time I got to spend here on earth with my friend. I am knowing my friend would love me to continue on and live my life to the fullest.

YOUR TURN - Have at it. Bookmark this section so you can revisit it as often as needed. Don't be surprised if you have repeats, write them all down.

DATE	STATEMENT	REPLACEMENT

DATE	**STATEMENT**	**REPLACEMENT**

Do you have a moment—or perhaps two or three—in your life that lingers over you like a chemical addiction? Do you find yourself re-enacting past situations with different people? Have you ever felt an uncontrollable bubbling in your body, a change in your breathing pattern, only to end up in another unwelcome situation, like a heated argument?

If so, take a moment to write it down below. Try to recall one or two instances from your past that might have served as the catalyst for this "chemical addiction." Keep your list brief—just one or two occurrences.

This exercise is not about dredging up past traumas but about recognizing patterns and understanding the emotions tied to them. By identifying the feelings associated with these moments, you can learn to anticipate them and replace them with new, empowering emotions.

Exercise #4 - THE ADDICTION

INITIAL SITUATION	AGE RANGE	REPEAT SITUATION AFTER CHEMICAL RUSH	AGE RANGE
Witnessing mother's physical abuse	5-10		

Your turn to dive in.

INITIAL SITUATION	AGE RANGE	REPEAT SITUATION AFTER CHEMICAL RUSH	AGE RANGE

Can you imagine all the things we do to ourselves—and the things we believe about ourselves—that carry no validity, and then wonder why our lives are so screwed up? If I just had more money. If I just had the career I wanted. We've all been there. It's very easy to look outside for external fixes. I bet we all know at least one person—or know of one person—who we thought had it all, and yet took their own life.

The fixes can never come from outside the self. Having millions of dollars and the freedom to do whatever you want in life won't help the broken child who lost a parent at a young age and is still longing for someone to love them.

Having witnessed all that her mother went through gave Dee an unmatched and unbelievable determination to win. She was tired, broken—but not willing to give up. She needed to continue to fight the good fight.

But why fight? Why did it have to be a struggle? Dee was conditioned from an early age to believe that "her life" was a struggle. All of the not-enough-isms she faced over the years added up to a journey full of hardship.

"If it wasn't for bad luck, we'd have no luck at all." That was a phrase she grew up hearing. Can you imagine hearing that on a consistent basis? That toxic phrase has struggle written all over it.

STOP THE MADNESS!

Only when she finally had enough, could Dee change all of it.

Exercise #5 – HONORING YOU

If you hang in there long enough, you can often find value in even the most unpleasant experiences. Looking back, how do you think the negative situations you've faced have made you stronger?

Take a moment to honor yourself. If you can, stand in front of a mirror, give yourself a big hug, and pat yourself on the back. Then, say to yourself:

Good job, [your name]. I am so proud of you. Thank you for hanging in there and turning lemons into lemonade. You've done an amazing job.

Feel free to write more below if you'd like to expand on this moment of self-honor.

_____

_____

_____

_____

_____

_____

_____

_____

_____

_____

_____

_____

_____

_____

_____

It's time for a gratitude break

Repeat the affirmation until you feel an uplifting, good feeling energy shift.

(Feel free to choose one or do them all)

* * *

I am grateful that today I place my attention where I want my energy to go. I've changed my mindset, and now my life has changed. The process of change requires me to be conscious of my unconscious self. I do this by focusing on things that have a high vibration and transmit great energy, bringing back more of the same. Today, I shift my perspective. I am so grateful that I see my life, and all those who are a part of it, as beacons for Team "Me." I am excited that they have all conspired to guide me, in a loving way, toward my highest good.

Terrah Bennett Smith

* * *

Don't let the fear of the time it will take to accomplish something stand in the way of your doing it. The time will pass anyway; we might as well put passing time to the best possible use.

Earl Nightingale

* * *

I am so happy and grateful that I courageously live each day of my life utilizing every talent I have. I am so happy and grateful that I enjoy every moment of my life, filling it with all the wonderful talents, ideas, and gifts I have been blessed with, and I am thankful that I get to share it with the world on a daily basis.

Terrah Bennett Smith

* * *

I Am So Happy And Grateful That I Have Shifted To A Higher Frequency And I Am Now Living And Manifesting A Much Better Life For Myself.

Bob Proctor

* * *

Embarrassment lasts a moment. Regrets lasts a lifetime. Never make permanent decisions on temporary feelings. A lot can change because you were embarrassed by it.

Terrah Bennett Smith

* * *

You are not making the change because you are a bad person and you are doing it wrong. You make changes because you Love yourself and you want to improve the quality of your life.

Louise Hay

* * *

I am so thankful that I woke up this morning and everything else is profit. I am truly blessed that I am living in the right now of my life and aligning with all the beauty that surrounds me.

Terrah Bennett Smith

* * *

n Act Two of life, we explore how our thoughts and energies correlate with the realities we manifest. You'll dive deeper into Dee's experiences and understand why writing this book and sharing her journey is so important. We'll also examine what it means to replace old patterns and reprogram for a better future.

***

Scene #1

THE BEAT DOWN

Beatings, beatings, and more beatings—oh my!

The origin of one of Dee's deepest pain sources can be traced back to when she was around four years old. Dee never fully understood when or why her father began abusing her mother, but once he started, the violence continued throughout most of their marriage.

Her tiny body was no match for her 6'1" father's wrath against her 5'3" mother. But that didn't matter to Dee—because if she didn't step in to protect her mother, who would?

Witnessing her sweet, petite mother endure physical abuse at the hands of her father became the blueprint for Dee's subconscious craving to mimic those same behaviors. She became almost obsessive about keeping her mother safe. Most of Dee's waking hours were consumed with concern for her mother's well-being. She would sit at the kitchen window, watching for her mom to walk up the long street and into the building, holding her breath until she heard the key in their front door.

Dee learned to fight by trying to protect her mom. Jumping into fights to defend her began at an early age and continued for years. The only relief Dee felt was when she was out playing with friends, momentarily distracted from her constant worry.

As the abuse continued, Dee's resentment toward her father deepened. Though he never directed his violence at his children, Dee felt every blow her mother endured. The trauma festered inside her. Her father, Lee, was a functioning alcoholic. Most days, he would return from work, have a few drinks—then a few more—and spiral into rage. He was an unhappy man, burdened by the lingering effects of his time in the army and the challenges of being an African American man in a racist society. Only he and God knew the full extent of his pain.

Still, his decision to unleash that pain on his small-framed wife infuriated, confused, and terrified Dee. It was the root of her severe trauma for years to come. His behavior was deeply wrong.

The more the beatings happened, the more Dee felt it was her duty to help. I'll spare you the details of the horrific pain her mother endured, but it was not unusual for him to casually walk past her and slap her across the face. She simply took it. Dee lived in constant anxiety whenever her father was around—a feeling surely dwarfed by what her mother experienced.

One late afternoon, everything came to a head. Dee walked into the kitchen to check on her mother and froze as she saw her father holding her mother's head out of the kitchen window, a butcher knife at her throat.

"Don't do it, Daddy! Don't do it!" Dee screamed, shaking with fear. "Oh God, please help my mother!"

Though terrified, Dee couldn't move. Thankfully, her father eventually let her mother go.

The next day, Dee begged her mother to let her stay home from school, terrified to leave her alone. Instead, her mother instructed her to take a note to the housing authority police. That school day felt endless. Damn— where were cell phones when you needed them?

Eventually, Dot filed for divorce. She never let her ex-husband back into their lives, and Dee was ecstatic. She didn't care if she ever saw him again. Finally, the beatings stopped—for now, at least. While her father's absence brought some comfort, the neural connection had already formed. That blueprint of physical abuse had become a subconscious part of Dee's life.

Her body began to crave abusive interactions. While most young girls dreamed of meeting their prince charming and riding off into the sunset, Dee's fantasies, though similar at first, always ended in violence. In her recurring daydreams, she and her partner would start off lovingly, enjoying life in a cozy two-bedroom townhouse. But by the end, they would be at each other's throats—literally. The fantasies felt so real, they seemed to be happening in real time. The more she imagined them, the more deeply ingrained they became.

Dot, Dee's mother, had 12 siblings and was especially close to the women in the family. Raised to believe in unconditional support for family, Dot didn't hesitate to become the legal guardian for her deceased sister's daughter or to take in her younger sister Louisa and Louisa's three sons after they were evicted. Suddenly, Dot's three-bedroom, one-bathroom apartment housed two adults, seven children, and a grandmother who frequently stayed for long stretches of time.

Dee and her siblings had strict rules and responsibilities, with household chores being non-negotiable. Failure to complete them came with consequences. However, Louisa had a far more lenient approach to parenting her sons, leaving them to their own devices and exempting them from chores.

Dee's two eldest cousins were close in age to her and her older sister. Angel, the middle son, was just a few months older than Dee and had a notoriously stubborn streak. On one particular day, his defiance came to a head. Taking out the trash to the incinerator seemed like a simple task, but Angel was determined not to do it. Dee's mother, Dot, wasn't having it, and his refusal escalated into a physical scuffle.

Right there, in the middle of the 14th-floor hallway, Angel fought with Dot while his mother, Louisa, sat in the apartment, doing and saying nothing. Dee's protective instincts immediately kicked in. "Stop! Somebody help my mother! Help!" she screamed. But no one came to Dot's rescue—except Dee. Eventually, the adrenaline simmered down, and everyone returned to their neutral emotional states.

A few weeks after the altercation with her nephew, Dot found herself in another heated conflict—this time with her sister, Louisa. Their argument turned into an all-out fistfight that resulted in the police being called. That incident was the breaking point for Dot. She demanded that Louisa and her sons leave her home.

There was a clear connection between Dot's conflict with her sister, her fight with her nephew, and her choice in an abusive husband. Despite the closeness Dot shared with her siblings, their childhood was rife with verbal abuse and frequent physical altercations. This history created a blueprint for abuse long before Dot met and married Lee. Otherwise, she likely wouldn't have attracted someone like him.

While Lee's estrangement from his family makes it hard to pinpoint the origin of his own pain, the fact that he is estranged speaks volumes."

Now, some people might say, "That doesn't give him the right to put his hands on her." Of course, it doesn't. But this book isn't about blaming others—it's about how *we* take responsibility for our lives and make changes to things we no longer want as part of our journey.

Providing for her three children on her modest salary—while often receiving no alimony or child support from Lee—Dot struggled to make ends meet. Years of not having enough, worrying about her children's well-being, and enduring emotional and physical abuse took their toll. Over time, Dot became withdrawn. She would sit at the kitchen window for hours, staring out while sipping a can of Ballantine Beer, one of her favorites. Perhaps the buzz from the alcohol dulled the edge of her pain.

Dot never spoke of her feelings—not to her siblings, not to anyone. She bottled it all inside, which was heartbreaking for Dee to witness.

'TIL DEATH

Dee was 16 years old when she watched her aunt Martha assist her mother in packing a bag for what was supposed to be a weekend stay in the hospital. But this time was different. It was as if her mother knew she wasn't coming back—and she never did.

Dot was well-loved in the community. Besides working at the school, she helped neighborhood kids get involved in the performing arts. But Dee had no idea just how cherished her mother was until the day of her funeral.

As the limousine turned the corner near the funeral home, Dee's eyes filled with tears. Staring out the window, she gasped, *Oh my goodness… what's going on?*

The sight was surreal: a massive line of people stretched around the block, leading to the funeral home's entrance. The scene resembled fans eagerly waiting to meet their favorite celebrity. As they drew closer, Dee realized the crowd was made up of people who had come to pay their respects to her mother.

Overwhelmed with emotion, Dee cried. The outpouring of love was both special and comforting.

Dee carried her mother's death as a personal responsibility—not because she believed she had caused it, but because she felt she had failed to prevent it. For years, she grappled with yet another version of her "not enough-isms":

If only I had taken better care of her. If I had been better at fighting, I could have protected her.

These thoughts plagued Dee, digging a deeper and deeper hole of guilt and regret.

✳ ✳ ✳

Scene #2

DELUXE APARTMENT IN THE SKY

Dee and her siblings moved in with their aunts, eventually leaving the Bronx for Manhattan. This was a step up. This time, they were living in an upscale high-rise building with a security guard who screened visitors before allowing entry. The building housed a mix of full-rent tenants and those who were subsidized. Dee's family fell into the latter category, though no one knew—well, perhaps until now. Regardless, walking in and out of that building, Dee reveled in the feeling of living in the lap of luxury.

Taking long walks became a therapeutic ritual for Dee. Armed with her Walkman, she used the time to clear her cluttered thoughts. In her twenties and still living at home, she wrestled with a slight depression. There were no immediate financial prospects that would allow her to move out and into the type of safe, luxurious, midtown Manhattan high-rise she dreamed of—a building with a doorman and the same level of comfort she had grown accustomed to.

Dee wasn't spoiled; she simply had standards. Deep down, she knew any move she made should be a step up or, at the very least, lateral—but never a step down.

One day, while walking through Washington Square Park on her way to meet her photographer and review her photo proofs, Dee had a strange encounter. A random man broke off from a conversation with a group of people and called out to her:

"Excuse me! Excuse me!"

Dee ignored him, as she often did with strangers in the city. But then he called out again:

"Excuse me! Is your birthday June 29th?"

Now he had her attention. Dee stopped for a second, instinctively grabbing her fanny pack, suspecting he might have stolen her wallet. But she quickly realized that was impossible—he was at least twenty feet away. Confused, concerned, yet a little curious, she cautiously nodded and said, "Yes, it is."

The man began rattling off what he saw:

"You're going to get married by the water. You'll have one child, then twins. You're going to be on television, and your life is about to change."

Then, just as abruptly, he turned back to his conversation.

Dee, a bit shaken, continued walking. She couldn't shake the interaction from her mind but chose not to speak of it for many years. Still, the moment lingered in her thoughts as she made her way to the photographer's studio.

While waiting for her photographer to finish with another client, Dee began browsing a bookshelf. One book in particular caught her eye: *You Can Heal Your Life* by Louise Hay. Perhaps it was the title that resonated.

Skimming through a few pages, Dee felt the words speak directly to her, as if they were written specifically for her experiences.

On her way home, she stopped at the nearest spiritual store and purchased the book—and the cassette tape. Yes, cassette. Dee played that tape on her Walkman for at least two weeks straight, flipping between side one and side two on repeat. The only time her headphones weren't glued to her ears was when she was at work or in the shower.

Dee was on a mission to change her life. Though she didn't see immediate results, she felt a deep knowing that she was headed in the right direction and preparing for a significant shift. She kept working on herself, embracing the process and even enjoying it.

Dee had been asking for her life to change but had no idea where to begin. What she didn't realize was that the transformation had already started.

DATING LIFE

Shawn, boyfriend number one, was Dee's first silent lesson. Dee and Shawn went away for a weekend to a friend's beach house. Still living at home with her aunts, who had taken over raising her and her siblings after her mother passed away, Dee saw this weekend getaway with her boyfriend as a welcomed, grown-up experience. The two prepared for what they thought would be a fun and innocent trip.

But for someone with Dee's history, time alone playing the role of an "adult" couple was the beginning of a deeper revelation. Yes, it was just a weekend—a short-term getaway—but Dee's mind blurred the lines between reality and a make-believe world that mimicked a husband and wife in their home. The chemical rush began to surface.

Stop! Stop! Cut it out, Dee!

Shawn's pleas fell on deaf ears. Dee was so consumed by her verbal and physical outburst that Shawn might as well have been talking to himself.

"Get off me!" she yelled as Shawn tried his best to avoid her blows. "Leave me alone! Get off of me!" she continued to scream.

Shawn wasn't the violent type, so all he could do was hold her until the "spell" passed. This would be the first time Dee experienced the chemical rush in full force. Like an addict after a fix, once Dee had exhausted the madness, she seemed calm and satisfied. Neither of them said much that evening; both were unsure of what had just happened.

Breaking the silence, Shawn finally asked, "Are you okay?"

Dee had no idea what had transpired. All she knew was that it felt weird as hell. The evening gave way to dawn without another word shared between them.

Let's call him Rick.

Some years later, before moving to Los Angeles, Dee met Rick while walking from the train station. Initially, their relationship was purely platonic. They bonded over their shared love for the arts, especially acting, and eventually became close friends.

During their hangouts, some of Dee's friends, who also knew her sister, often remarked on how much Rick resembled her. Dee agreed. The resemblance was striking. To her, it simply meant Rick was cute—because her sister was, too.

Slowly but surely, their friendship turned intimate. Dee liked Rick... somewhat. But she wasn't deeply invested in the relationship, and when the opportunity to pack up and move to sunny California arose, she jumped at the chance without hesitation. Leaving him behind barely crossed her mind.

"A fresh new start," she thought.

But as they say, *you can run, but you can't hide.* Wherever Dee went, she took herself—and all her unresolved emotions—with her.

SUNNY CALI

Arriving in California on a hot sunny day, Dee immediately knew this was the place for her. It was January, and people were walking around in shorts and flip-flops. A new place meant a new start, and being tied down wasn't part of the plan, so she broke things off with Rick. Dee's acting career was on the rise. She booked her first television series role and was part of a three-girl recording group. Boyfriend? Who had the time?

Dee took her work seriously and was excited to continue her spiritual journey. Determined to maintain the momentum of positive changes in her life, she contacted the number listed in her "You Can Heal Your Life" book and discovered a weekly spiritual group led by Dr. Linda Logan. This group was ideal for Dee, allowing her to meet like-minded individuals and continue her journey of growth.

"You should come to my church on Sunday. I'm the assistant Reverend, and they'll teach you more of what you've learned here. I think you'll like it," Dr. Logan said. Dee eagerly replied, "City of Angels?" She was ready. Anywhere she could deepen her self-work was exciting. Dee made new friends through both her acting and spiritual circles.

Rick and Dee continued to talk. He expressed interest in visiting to see life in Los Angeles, and Dee was fine with that. After all, they were "friends."

Two weeks later, Dee and Kat, a friend from the spiritual group, attended a new spiritual center. The service was moderate, the music passable, but the after-service reception was a highlight. While enjoying refreshments, a random woman approached Dee and said, "Stop worrying about your finances. Everything will turn out fine." She proceeded to share startlingly accurate details about Dee's life, including her mother's passing during Dee's teens. The woman also said, "Someone with the initial 'R' is coming to visit, and it will be the hardest yet best lesson of your life." It took Dee a while to connect the "R" to Rick.

Fast-forward six months (give or take). R had moved to Cali, and Dee was somehow in the throes of a live-in boyfriend. It wasn't long before the appearance of sweet turned to sour. Was it a coincidence that Dee looked just like her mother, and R looked a lot like Dee's sister, who looked like their father? Bam! And bam again! Dee had manifested her childhood. Interesting, huh? All those daydreams, focusing on the abuse and fantasizing about being physically abused— all that energy helped to create her current scenario.

Luckily for Dee, it wasn't as physically abusive as her mother's. Her experience was more emotional, with a few physical instances and mild choking. Hmmmm. Mild choking— is there such a thing?

The other very weird "coincidence," if you want to call any of this that, was that they lived in a two-bedroom, two-story townhome, which resembled the one in Dee's daydreams. WOW! Could it be that she focused on it so much that not only did the players reappear, but also the location? The pain bodies were surfacing, and things were about to get real. And still, at that time, Dee was unable to see the correlation.

The abuse went on for about seven months. This tough Bronx girl was so broken and confused— and too embarrassed to share what she was going through with anyone— that she found writing in a journal was her form of therapy.

"Dear God. How did I get here? I could never believe someone with my toughness could end up in this situation. You know me, God. I am a New York City chick who no one messes with."

This was her daily rant to the universe. She was so totally unaware that her experiences were connected to the energetic tree she had planted some years ago. Who'd've thunk?

And just for clarity—the abuse was not only reserved for her boyfriends; it would rear its head in other relationships.

This would be the beginning of the end of her bout with abusive relationships. All the books and tapes, and her newfound spirituality, offered her tools on how to replace her old patterns and help her align with what she truly wanted for herself. But like any change, you have to go through what you no longer want to get to what you do want. It was time to say goodbye to those old habits. She felt like a junkie going through withdrawals. Literally. It was painful. Saying goodbye to something she had a long-standing relationship with felt like a guttural release.

She left Rick one day after having an out-of-body experience. Yes, another one of many surreal moments she would experience.

It was nearing the Christmas holiday, and the two of them got into a heated argument over Dee needing to stay in Los Angeles longer than anticipated. This was at the request of her agents. Now, why this was an issue with Rick was confusing to Dee, because they were going home to two very different states.

One thing led to another, and Dee found herself in a chokehold. Something clicked in her head as she played back a previous conversation they had, where he convinced her that he never initiated hitting her—it was only in defense. This time, she wanted clarity.

When he got close to her face, and just before his hands reached her neck, Dee placed her hands behind her back and locked them. She needed proof that she never struck him first, and she got it.

The funniest thing was, during this whole escapade, Dee felt like she had an angel walking her through the necessary steps so that she could clearly see her life. After Rick loosened his grip on her neck, he proceeded into the bathroom, closing the door and turning up the music.

Dee was left leaning against the outside of the door, crying. Then—boom!—she had an out-of-body experience. She had only had one once before, where she thought she was dying. But this time, she felt safe, so she just watched herself cry.

Once the experience was over, Dee walked to the bedroom and wrote on a piece of paper, *"I will not be back this time."*

She proceeded downstairs to her already packed suitcase, which had remained in the living room from the night before. Yeah, she had left him several times, but it never stuck. This time, Dee kept her promise to herself. She did not come back. But the withdrawals were deep. Many days and nights were spent in her parked car, crying.

It felt like she was dying. Well, technically, *a part of her was.* Dee was saying goodbye to her long relationship with her energetic, abusive monster.

Taking the steps to leave Rick and not return was one of the hardest things she had to do. Aimlessly driving around in her car, crying, Dee worked overtime to not give in to the chemical cravings that were running amok inside of her. All she knew to do was ball up in a fetal position and cry, hoping the cravings would eventually subside— and they did.

Dee's flight back to L.A. from visiting her family for the Christmas holiday was on New Year's Eve. Such an interesting day to choose to come back to her now homeless situation. Nonetheless, there she was at LAX, roaming the airport, trying to figure out where she was going to stay.

Not well thought out, Dee. Wouldn't it have made sense to stay in NY until she figured things out? Yeah… but no.

Deep down, she knew she needed to close out the chapter, and the place to do that was not NY. She needed to return and get back to her growth work.

Dee stopped at an airport payphone, put her quarter in, and— not really knowing why— dialed Rick. The conversation was brief. Dee was in victim mode, so any words that followed *hello* were not for her highest good.

"I don't have anywhere to go," she spouted into the phone.

Maybe subconsciously she knew those words would evoke something that would assist her in some way— and they did.

Rick responded with, *"Well, it was your choice to leave, so don't blame me."*

Dee immediately hung up the phone and called a friend, Kat, who offered her a place to stay for as long as she needed.

Dee had several friends who supported her during this time. This transitional period forced her to set aside her pride and fully embrace the love and support they offered. Graciously, she accepted their kindness, staying in their homes until she was strong enough to stand on her own again.

She would eventually secure a two-bedroom, two-story townhouse. With no money but unshakable faith, she declared, "Work it out, God!" Within a week, she booked a television job that allowed her to move in.

Dee returned to Rick's to retrieve her belongings. A neighbor confessed she often heard Dee crying and was relieved she'd left. Rick professed his desire to rekindle their relationship. Dee's response was clear: "Then you're sick and need help." She thanked him silently and closed that chapter.

As Dee continued moving from relationship to relationship, she paid close attention to when those chemical surges crept in—and took full ownership of them. Anytime she felt uncomfortable or was made to feel uncomfortable by someone's words or actions, she looked in the mirror. Pointing the finger at others became useless; to Dee, it meant *she* had work to do.

The more she applied herself and worked toward clarity, the more signs of clarity she received. As she delved deeper into understanding herself, the workings of the universe, and the law of attraction, she became increasingly connected to what seemed like supernatural occurrences.

Dee was never much of a gym person, but she loved exercises that felt fun. Anything outdoors suited her—except swimming, of course. It was a way for her to blend physical activity with spirituality, meditation, and staying in shape. She wanted her mind, body, and spirit to be in sync. Dee was disciplined that way—or maybe just vain.

Many people admired her work ethic. She read her books, worked out regularly, and was often seen as a life and fitness coach. So why not make it official? To supplement her income, she decided to get her personal trainer certification.

One day, while training a client, Dee faced yet another life-enlightening experience.

Cee was a middle-aged woman who wanted to lose a few pounds but didn't enjoy exercising, so Dee tailored her workout regimen around activities she loved—walking being one of them. It was one of those blazingly sunny Santa Monica days as Dee and Cee took their usual warm-up walk.

Suddenly, Cee yelled, *"Watch out, Dee!"*

Dee didn't remember the actual impact, but she recalled seeing the shape of her body in a dotted formation.

"Holy shit!" she muttered, most likely to herself.

As she was helped off the ground, her senses returned. Yet, she was so mesmerized by what she had just witnessed that she barely registered the fact that she had been hit by a car. The whole experience felt strangely peaceful—no injuries, no lasting bodily damage.

She spent the rest of the day pondering what had happened. *Was I hallucinating?* No, she didn't believe so. But the few people she confided in tried their best to convince her otherwise. Still, Dee *knew* what she had seen was real. It was something other-dimensional, something unexplainable. It would take years before she finally got her answer.

One day, as she watched a television monitor, a video of Deepak Chopra played. He was explaining what happens when someone gets hit by a car. Dee's attention locked in.

Onscreen, Chopra demonstrated how, upon impact, a person's body transforms into a series of dots.

"That's what I saw!" Dee shouted. *"I knew I wasn't crazy!"*

At that moment, she realized she had tapped into some deeper connection—something beyond ordinary understanding. The mere opportunity to *have* that experience was proof that she could no longer settle for being mediocre.

Other-dimensional experiences continued to show up in Dee's life. They weren't always comfortable, but they carried a clear message: **RELAX AND STAY ALIGNED—YOU'RE ALWAYS OKAY.**

Dee had just completed a starring role in a pilot for a new television series and was waiting to see if the network would pick it up. In the meantime, she needed to find work. A close friend, who worked as a stand-in on a popular network show, offered to put in a recommendation for her.

Dee wasn't sure why she thought this job would be a good fit. Being still and focusing when she wasn't actively stimulated was still one of her biggest challenges—and a stand-in job was *anything but* stimulating. Yet, when the offer came, she felt obligated to take it. Little did she know, this job would serve as another major awakening.

It was time to go back to work, but on this particular day, Dee could barely muster the energy to stand in for *anyone*. After all, she had just wrapped a pilot where *she* had a stand-in. Still, she had given her word. To lift her spirits, she dressed in her favorite energy color—orange. From head to toe, she looked like a citrus fruit. Even her laptop was orange.

The producer/writer of the show loved incorporating musical numbers, and this episode was no different. Seated in the back of the auditorium, Dee tried her best to ignore the sting of envy as she watched actresses of her caliber rehearsing a dance routine on stage.

Inside, she seethed. *I'm a good actor, singer, and dancer too. Why do they get to do what they love?*

This was hard—especially today. All she wanted was to go home and cry.

Behind her, the craft services table was filled with snacks. Instead of sitting there sulking, Dee decided, *Well, if I can't join them, I might as well eat.*

She headed to the table, scanning the selection, when a crew member approached the far end, busy making a sandwich. No words were exchanged.

And then—out of nowhere—she heard it.

"GO DOWN FRONT."

Dee immediately turned toward the crew member, but he was still focused on stacking layers of meat and cheese onto his bread.

Her heart pounded. *Who said that?*

She looked around, but aside from the two of them, no one else was nearby. Panic crept in. *I don't know who said that, so I'm not moving. People will think I'm crazy, listening to these random voices.*

She tried to brush it off, redirecting her attention back to the food.

"I SAID, GO DOWN FRONT!"

The voice was louder now. More commanding.

Dee was beyond freaked out. But this time, she was too afraid *not* to listen.

Slowly, cautiously, she made her way toward the front of the auditorium and took a seat in the middle of the eighth row.

Why are you listening to the crazy voices in your head? she questioned herself. *Why are you even sitting here?*

Less than a minute later, one of the actresses, Loretta—whom Dee had met during a guest-starring role but barely knew—called out to her.

"You're a choreographer, right?"

Dee hesitated. She had trained in dance and could handle most styles, but a *choreographer*? Not exactly.

Still, she responded, *"Ahh… huh."*

Loretta turned to one of the executive producers, Ed, and said, *"She's a choreographer, and we could use some help up here."*

Ed made his way over. *"You're a choreographer?"*

Again, with hesitation, Dee replied, *"Ahh… huh."*

Then he asked, *"Are you in the union?"*

Dee thought quickly. *I know there's a dancer's union, but I can't think of the name. But hey, I'm part of the Screen Actors Guild, and that's a union.*

So, once again, she answered, *"Ahh… huh."*

Ed nodded. *"If we hire you and pay you your rate, would you be okay choreographing without credit?"*

This time, with confidence, Dee replied, *"Of course, no worries. I'd be happy to."*

She had no desire to choreograph beyond this gig, so credit wasn't important.

For the rest of the season, production called on her whenever a musical number needed staging. That day marked the end of her stand-in career—and the beginning of rediscovering the *in-charge* person she had buried as a child.

These other-dimensional experiences were teaching her a powerful lesson: As long as she stayed aligned and in tune with her truth, she would *always* be taken care of.

Worrying was a choice. A waste of energy.

And as she continued doing her inner work, clarity arrived in all sorts of ways. Even through contrast.

Dee's journey was filled with trials, lessons, and growth. Each experience—from her relationships to her career to her spiritual awakenings—served as a stepping stone toward a fuller understanding of herself and her purpose. She learned to trust the process, embrace change, and align with the universe's plan for her life.

Important Recap Before Moving Forward with Dee's Manifestations:

- Dee struggled with sinus issues and daily nosebleeds, which her parents attempted to treat with a makeshift Southern remedy.
- Dee looked just like her mother, while her sister resembled their father, Lee.
- Dee would lie awake at night, fantasizing about having a boyfriend—her prince. But instead of him arriving on a white horse, her prince would slap her around before they made up and enjoyed each other's company.
- Dee fantasized about her prince slapping her for no apparent reason. Their arguments seemed to come out of nowhere, because that was the program she was running.
- Dee's fantasy was so vivid that she even envisioned the home they would live in: a two-bedroom, two-story townhouse with a washer and dryer in the unit.
- Dee somehow felt that she hadn't done a good enough job of protecting her mother.

* * *

Scene #3

THE MANIFESTATIONS

Dee's childhood experiences and fantasies were now in full-blown manifestation mode. She had no idea how these experiences and her energetic participation had designed the blueprint for what was to come. She did not realize that every time she shared the story or emotionally played it out in her mind, a chemical response would converge and conform into a habit. This habit would inevitably rev up at unexpected moments, forcing her to act upon its presence. It was no different from an addict needing a fix and going in search of an insidious street drug to satisfy their chemical addiction.

These uncontrollable urges had taken up dwelling in Dee, carrying out their mission well into her adulthood. She was unaware of what these feelings were called or why she was experiencing them, but at some point, she came to understand that the urges were always followed by an experience associated with pain. That much was clear. However, when you have no point of reference, the writing on the wall often seems written with invisible ink.

The Manifestations from the Reprogramming

For Dee, the process was not as cut-and-dry as it might sound. There were still steps and contrasts she needed to work through. If she was going to shift this once and for all, she had to deprogram and replace every pain body that reared its ugly head.

Excited about the prospect of the new Dee, she went into action. She began to date with a purpose. It's not as cold as it sounds—she needed to observe each relationship from a third-person perspective. Dee paid close attention to the things her partners said to her early in the relationship and to how she reacted and felt around them. This was her mission, and it worked.

She noticed that each relationship was better than the one before—or rather, that she was becoming better in each of them. Dee was able to see early on what she was no longer willing to tolerate in herself, in that person, or in the situation. She nipped it in the bud immediately.

Dee also learned that abuse comes in many forms: physical, psychological, emotional, sexual, or financial. Purposely withholding or enforcing pain in any of these areas constitutes abuse. For Dee, what started as physical abuse eventually turned verbal and emotional, with the long-standing form being financial. It took years, but she found her way out of them all.

As we go through life on a daily basis, we are bound to encounter people or situations that may cause us pain. The key is to have tools to move through them expeditiously. That's what this work offers. Contrast never goes away; we simply learn to manage it. Life would be quite dull without it.

Remember the nosebleeds and the water faucet running over Dee's face as a remedy? This eventually manifested into a fear of drowning. At that early age, neither Dee nor her parents had any idea that she was in the process of forming a long-term relationship with this experience.

Dee's fear was so powerful that every time she found herself submerged in water deeper than her neck, she felt as though she was dying. Washing her hair became an unwelcome weekend chore. Dee would cry profusely whenever she had to immerse her head under the running shower. She would beg her mother to turn her around and hold her head the other way. Something as simple as washing out shampoo became a battle.

Her mother couldn't understand why Dee refused to simply bend forward and let the shower run down her face to rinse it out the easy way. But it wasn't simple for Dee—it was terrifying. The more she tried or was forced to do it, the more the fear cemented itself. Dee's brain had formulated those early experiences, locked them in, and set the tone for what would become many frightening water-related moments in her future.

Like her mother and father, Dee's choice in relationships—men in particular—reflected the patterns she had formed a childhood connection with. Physical abuse was the name of that pattern. They both unknowingly craved it, like the abusive junkies they had become. This made it extremely hard to rid themselves of its grip. Her parents attracted each other and fulfilled each other's magnetic needs. In much the same way, Rick and Dee were also a magnetic match. They remained connected until one of their desires to change became stronger than their need to stay the same.

You have the power to change direction at any time!

Now, let's tackle Dee's issue with drowning in the shower. Dee began practicing by immersing her face in the water for just a few seconds at a time during her showers. The first few attempts were petrifying for her. Slowly but surely, each time got a little easier. Now, she loves sticking her face into the water and feeling the warmth trickle down her body. One small step for mankind, one giant leap for Dee.

She has not yet overcome her fear of swimming, but she's getting closer to manifesting swimming lessons. That programming runs deep! Wish her luck.

Moving on to the "boyfriends"—or rather, relationships in general. When Dee eventually realized that abuse manifested itself in more ways than just the behavior of the men she dated, she began to examine everyone in her life and how their words and actions affected her. She approached each relationship with special care, determined to uncover and address any patterns of harm, no matter how subtle.

There are many more manifestations we could share, but I think you get the picture. The more you focus on anything, the longer you give energy to it, and best believe it will manifest. The exciting thing is that this works for both the good-feeling things and the not-so-good-feeling things. It's your choice. Pick the side of least resistance and go for it. I don't know about you, but I've finally chosen the good feelings, and my life has CHANGED!

Every opportunity to imagine your desired life sets that lifestyle in motion. Whether it's a mother or someone else who sets boundaries for you, perhaps a disliked boss, or a job you can't wait to leave—no matter the circumstances or individuals, no one can control what goes on in your head or the energy that emanates from you. So, although you might feel frustrated inside, it's important to hold onto the vision of the life you want and allow that energy to take flight. That's your little secret: "YOU" must be the catalyst for yourself. So, that mate, boss, or friend you feel is out of sync with you? They are actually a catalyst for the awakening of a lesson you need to learn.

People and situations come into your life as a reflection of your beliefs. This is a very hard pill for most of us to swallow. It's easy to point the finger and say, "You're the reason I am feeling, doing, or being this way." But in time, when you peel back the layers and reflect on the various people who come in and out of your life, you'll begin to see similarities in them—and how you are the sole consistent entity. You're the common denominator. Their purpose may not be clear in the beginning, so you might not catch the subtle message. But as you strengthen those muscles and begin to pay attention daily, you will start to see more and more what the reflection is trying to show you. When this happens, don't be mad—thank them for coming to show you "you."

Start today by being grateful that you understand the importance of the energy you emit and the need to place your attention in the direction of where you want that energy to go. Be grateful that, right now, you understand that the process of change requires you to be conscious of your unconscious self—and that you can only attract the good you desire by focusing on things that have high vibration and transmit great energy. This will inevitably bring more of the same back to you.

Somehow, Dee innately knew that when changing one's mindset, it's also important to engage the body and spirit. So, cleaning up her diet became paramount to living a high-vibrational lifestyle. What she didn't know was how food connected to her allergy issues. Simply changing her diet alleviated her sinus problems and sent those pesky nosebleeds packing. Done and done!

Claim it, reframe it, then aim it—in your new desired direction. That's Dee's personal mantra. Feel free to try it out. Maybe there's something or someone you'd like to get out of your life. Make it your own. "I claim you, but I disdain you, and now I aim you right into the trash." Visualize the process. The quicker you take ownership, the quicker you can move through it and rise to a higher vibration.

A BEAUTIFUL MIND

The movie *A Beautiful Mind* was an eye-opener for Dee. It connected so many additional dots for her. If you haven't seen it, I suggest you give it a watch. Russell Crowe's character was schizophrenic, and his inability to decipher reality from the people in his head wasn't so far from what most of us deal with on a regular basis. Dee's traumatic life experiences had taken up so much space in her subconscious that they often took control. At certain points, she felt powerless and, more often than not, succumbed to their emotions. There was a time when she believed she would never free herself from them. After watching this movie, Dee decided to identify them by name, which made them less mysterious and less controlling.

For Dee, certain patterns were easier to replace and took much less time. But there were others that were so deeply rooted that, even when it seemed she had defeated or replaced them, something as simple as a statement, a smell, or a visual could bring them right back to the forefront of her brain. It works according to what we feed it.

Dee worked diligently to stay ahead of the chemical surges. Like Russell Crowe's character, they seemed to appear out of nowhere and often caught her off guard. She knew the only way to get in front of them was to do her daily work. Meditation, gratitude journaling, keeping her vibrations high, monitoring the company she kept, and getting into the habit of immediately replacing any lower-vibration thoughts or energy—this had to become her routine.

YOU'VE BEEN PROMOTED TO MANAGER

Once you begin this journey, you'll have to manage your thoughts on a daily basis. There was a time when Dee was manifesting everything she wanted. Because she spent so much time alone, she worked on herself more hours than not. She had vision boards around her home, photos of herself stuck to her television, mirrors, and even in her car. It felt good. After a few consistent years of this practice, she started to see the manifestations pour in, what she thought was on a regular basis. Her career began to bloom, money was flowing, and she had her dream apartment. She enjoyed her new life but somehow got so caught up that she neglected to keep up the work that had brought her to this place. It wasn't long before Dee developed a false sense of security, and it would take just one incident, one challenging day, to throw her back into the clutches of contrasts. It's almost as if they lie dormant, waiting for the opportunity to strike. Just when your guard is down, here they come. That's why it's important to do daily work. No one can physically carry a vision board around with them. Can you imagine seeing someone walk around with their vision board in front of their face to remind them of where their focus should be? Life happens. Things happen. Although vision boards are a wonderful tool, they have no power against those pesky chemical surges. They don't help when the addiction starts to talk to your mind about what you say you don't want. Nothing and no one changes until you change your energy. So having an inner vision board—one that you keep in the forefront of your mind—is the key. It will help you manage "you," which is important to keep "you" on track.

LOOKING FOR THE BAD IN SITUATIONS

What does it mean to wait for the other shoe to drop? It's a mindset where we constantly anticipate negative outcomes, sometimes suspecting that someone may be plotting against us or trying to undermine our efforts. We've all experienced moments when a series of unfortunate events occurred. When this repeats itself often enough, our minds begin to doubt the possibility of positive outcomes, discouraging us from getting excited about things for fear that they'll take a downward spiral. This is why it's important to engage in self-reflection and personal growth. While it may not be possible to fix every challenge, self-awareness enables you to recognize and address your issues, manage them, and prevent them from being passed on.

WHY FORGIVE?

This can be a tough one sometimes. Depending on the situation, forgiveness can either take a toll on you or be as simple as pie. When it comes to a locked pattern, forgiveness has proven to be something most of us are less likely to do. How often do you hear someone who has been wronged say, "I forgive them," but in the back of their mind, you sense a desire for vindication? If that person faces a misfortune—for instance, they lose a bid on a job—there's a sense of "See, that's what they get." "God does not like ugly." Or you might hear, "I don't wish them harm, but I don't feel bad for them either." There's something about seeing the person who wronged you get a dose of their own medicine. It makes you feel better in that moment, but that's not truly forgiveness.

Taking you back to the story of Dee and Rick—some years later, they became really good friends. A few of Dee's friends, who knew their story, were baffled. "Why would you want to talk to him, after all he put you through?" When you understand that we are all here with lessons to learn, and that no one is in charge of our feelings but us, you realize that you can't continue to play the blame game and expect to grow.

WHO'S ACCOUNTABLE AGAIN?

It's said that we are one hundred percent responsible for the energy we put out. If something you want is taking a long time to manifest, it can only be because you are spending more time focused on the fact that it hasn't manifested than on its presence. Since we create through vibration, not actions, our job is to find the seed of the vibration we want to plant, water it, and then sit back and allow the universal forces to take care of the "HOW." *Acronym for - Helps On the Way!* - Thank you for that Dr. Linda Logan.

You—and only you—are responsible for your life choices and decisions.

$$* * *$$

That's a powerful reflection, and I believe we all have moments like this. Sometimes, the things we desire take longer to materialize than we expect, and by the time they do, we might not immediately connect them to the original dream. It can be especially true when we're caught up in the process of growth or transformation. I can imagine it must be a challenge to reconnect with those moments, especially when they seem to come full circle much later in life.

Do you recall any childhood dreams you had that you didn't see come true right away, or perhaps ones that took on a different shape when they finally did manifest? It might be a great exercise to look back and reconnect the dots—both for things you want to change and for the incredible power you've harnessed along the way!

Exercise #6 - POWERHOUSE ME.

DESIRED DREAM/FANTASY PAST	MANIFESTATION
Live in a nice hi-rise apartment building	Moved from the Bronx to midtown Manhattan into a hi-rise building with security guard, and a view overlooking the city. It's the best feeling in the world as I walk through the entrance and I'm greeted with a hello from the doorman. And I thought having milk machines in the lobby were high-class living.

It's your turn, so have at it.

DESIRED DREAM/FANTASY PAST	MANIFESTATION

Exercise #7 - POSITIVE RANT SESSION

I am so grateful that money comes to me in increasing quantities through multiple sources on a continuous basis, doing what I love.

I am so grateful for my comfortable bed.

I am so thankful that I woke up this morning.

It's your turn. Don't think about it. Let it rip from you. It's okay to repeat the same ones, as long as you feel it, keep them coming.

_____

_____

_____

_____

_____

_____

_____

_____

_____

_____

_____

_____

_____

_____

_____

_____

It's time for a gratitude break #2

*Repeat the affirmation until you feel an uplifting,
good feeling energy shift.*

(Feel free to choose one or do them all)

* * *

(Remember)

*Don't let anything stand in the way of you claiming and manifesting
the life that you choose rather than the life you have by default.*

Joy Page

* * *

(now repeat as an affirmation)

*I am grateful that have manifested the life that I have chosen for
myself and I chose to live my life on purpose and with positive intent.*

* * *

(Remember)

*The only successful manifestation is one which brings a change or
growth in consciousness. That is, it has manifested God, or revealed
him more fully as well as having manifested a form.*

David Spangler

* * *

(now repeat as an affirmation)

*Within me is the ability to manifest and attract everything that
I desire. I am so grateful that I am in alignment with
all things that are for my highest good.*

INTERMISSION

Grab a beverage, a snack and take a moment to for a quick overview before we go onto the last Act.

* * *

The Law of Attraction is REAL, y'all. What you put out, you can bet your bottom dollar it's coming back to you. Over the years, I have prided myself on being a giving person—almost to my own detriment. But my giving wasn't always from the best place. It's the Law of Attraction, so how and why we give is important. There's giving out of guilt, self-promotion, or giving out of love and support. I now only give when I'm moved to, because it's important that what I attract back mirrors what I've vibrated out. I'd like to give you something.

Below, I am sharing with you a real, life-shifting gift. You might already be familiar with this artist, but if not, you're in for a real treat. I have no rights to this music or connection to the artist, other than how his music served as a catalyst for change in my life—and I want that for you as well.

* * *

https://www.robertcoxon.com/preludetoinfinity
https://www.robertcoxon.com/cristalsilencel

* * *

Take a moment to close your eyes, or if you're not in a safe, private space, simply take a few deep breaths and turn inward. If you're able, put on your headphones (or earbuds) and play any selection from Robert Haig Coxon's *The Silent Path* (Prelude to Infinity) and/or *Crystal Silence* (The Silence Within) CDs (links below).

These CDs have high vibrational energy and will immediately evoke a positive feeling in your body. I'm sure any of his other CDs will provide the same vibrational uplift, but these two, for sure, did it for me. I'm hooked.

As you listen, envision. Keep your mind focused on the prize of gratitude. Don't worry too much about focusing on what you want to manifest. When you keep your mind on gratitude, you're on a high vibrational frequency, which is where all the good you desire resides. You can't help but align with your good and manifest it.

AND… WE'RE BACK!

Let's revisit those manifestations we talked about earlier in this act:

- Dee's nosebleeds and sinus issues, and how her parents' remedy affected her.
- How much Dee resembles her mother and her sister resembles her father.
- Dee's fantasies about abusive relationships.
- The townhome Dee fantasized about living in.
- The feeling that she did not do enough to help her mother.

MIND - BODY - SPIRIT

U p until now, we have been focusing on ridding ourselves of inner toxins. There are many levels of cleansing that need to take place in order to align with one's higher self. As we mentioned earlier, abuse comes in many forms—abuse of food, drugs, alcohol, laziness, clutter, etc. In this section, we focus on the body and spirit. Are you ready to bring it all together? Well then, let's continue.

*** *** ***

Scene #1

DETOXING - YOUR FOOD

Dee's journey to a healthier diet officially started in a backhanded sort of way. She had an aunt who introduced her family to organic eating, but her journey really kicked into full throttle when she started dating a guy who didn't eat meat at the time, so she followed suit. Who knew it would have a lasting effect on her life? But there's something about feeling healthier and saying goodbye to health issues that made going back to eating meat unappealing. Vegetarian and vegan lifestyles weren't as popular back then, which often made it difficult for a foodie like Dee to stay on track. Outside of tofu, tempeh, veggies, fruits, and legumes, options were limited. Most people who choose a vegetarian diet do it for the sanctity of animals, the planet, or health reasons—but not for something as frivolous as, "I'm dating a cute guy who's a vegetarian, so why not?" The longer Dee stayed on her meatless journey, the more she discovered additional benefits. She no longer had stomach cramping after eating, her severe sinus issues disappeared, no more daily nosebleeds, and she dropped about 10-15 pounds. She was already thin but enjoyed the new physical and emotional person she had become.

Making healthier eating choices had a multitude of benefits for her. For instance, she began fasting every weekend. From Friday to Sunday, she would cleanse her system with lemon water. She did this more as a spiritual practice than for cleansing purposes. The first month was challenging, but after thirty days, she managed it like a pro. She noticed that when she fasted, her energy level and mental clarity soared. Because water flushes out the kidneys and liver, it felt as though the food she had previously eaten was weighing her down. She cut out soft drinks and drank mostly juices, eventually replacing juices with lemon water. Detoxing helps to boost energy, rid the body of excess waste, aid in weight loss, build a stronger immune system, improve skin, promote healthy changes, clear thinking, a lighter feeling, anti-aging benefits, and improvement in overall well-being—these are just a few of the results Dee was blessed with.

Now, of course, at this time, Dee was living at home and didn't have to cook for her family. She was only responsible for feeding herself, so there was less temptation. If you're already feeling defeated, take a deep breath. We are not suggesting you stop eating meat or begin fasting. From her many failed attempts, Dee knew the importance of NOT trying to eliminate her favorite foods unless, of course, it's for health reasons. The mind seems to accept that challenge more easily when it's for health, making it easier to complete. Start by decreasing the amounts of those food items. It becomes easier to do this in increments, and eventually, when you start feeling amazing, you might choose to cut them out altogether. Another key factor is replacement. Just as we need to replace the thoughts we no longer want to think, it's no different with food. We are creatures of habit, so we have to form new habits by replacing the old and repeating the new. Eventually, the new diet will become your go-to.

Again, let's make this clear: I'm not suggesting anyone become a vegan or vegetarian, but what is being suggested is that you evaluate your food intake and perhaps make some adjustments. Try Meatless Mondays. Vegetable Tuesdays. No-Sweet Saturdays. Create a theme for yourself. A clogged body comes with a multitude of issues—sickness, disease, pain, mental exhaustion, etc. Ridding your body of the weighing-down toxins leaves you feeling good. It's an easy way to detox, and you will definitely feel better.

It's time for you to begin taking a look at what could be eliminated from your diet. Let's start with this past week. Write down your best recollection of everything you ate, and if you can, go back as far as you can remember from this past month and do the same. Even if you can't remember every item you've eaten, write down whatever you can recall. Pay close attention to when you dined out, what you ate, and how much you paid for your meal. Highlight all the items you could do without, even though you most likely won't want to. Do your research to see the value in eating them, read the labels, and, if necessary, find a replacement. Trust me, there are plenty of healthier, tasty alternatives, especially now in 2025.

Exercise #8 - YOU ARE WHAT YOU EAT

DAY	MEAL/ SNACKS/ DRINKS
Monday	
Tuesday	
Wednesday	
Thursday	
Friday	
Saturday	
Sunday	

WEEK TWO

DAY	MEAL/ SNACKS/ DRINKS
Monday	
Tuesday	
Wednesday	
Thursday	
Friday	
Saturday	
Sunday	

WEEK THREE

DAY	MEAL/ SNACKS/ DRINKS
Monday	
Tuesday	
Wednesday	
Thursday	
Friday	
Saturday	
Sunday	

WEEK FOUR

DAY	MEAL/ SNACKS/ DRINKS
Monday	
Tuesday	
Wednesday	
Thursday	
Friday	
Saturday	
Sunday	

***

Scene #2

DETOXING – YOUR CLOSET

So many of us have a closet, apartment, office, or car that reflects our clutter. Are you one of those people who, when company comes over, quickly thrust bags of unused stuff into your closets, promising to do a deep clean and get rid of it all once they leave? Or perhaps your closets are so full you barely remember what's in them. Often, external clutter reflects some type of internal clutter—a clog in the brain, perhaps. Let's focus on the closet specifically, but feel free to apply this to all areas of your external clutter.

How many things are in your closet that you never wear—or at least haven't worn in the past six months to a year? It's funny how we justify keeping an item with the idea that we'll want to wear it or need it sometime in the future. But usually, by the time an opportunity arises, you forget you have it and end up purchasing something new for the occasion. Purging your closet, although time-consuming and overall annoying to most, is quite liberating and opens up space.

Let's begin. Pick a day when you'll have the least interruptions. Plan out your meals in advance so you won't be distracted by hunger. Set a soothing atmosphere for yourself. Start by putting on some of your favorite music (purging closet music). Now pour a glass of something to drink—wine, iced tea, or simply some ice water. If you're really into setting the mood, light a few scented candles. The goal is to create a comforting environment while you begin the process of letting go. Have a bag for charity, friends, or family, or just get rid of anything you haven't worn in the last year.

You can also take it a few steps further and throw a "Let It Go" party. Invite your friends to declutter their closets and homes, organize a potluck, bring all the items, set them up around your house, and shop. No exchange of money. You'll be surprised at how many items you acquire that still have tags on them. This is one way to detox your closet and have big fun. When you hold onto things, you don't allow space to welcome new things into your life. It's like having your hand tightly closed—nothing can get out, and nothing can come in either.

Give it a try. However you decide to declutter, it puts you in a spirit of giving. Purging and letting items go is a form of giving, and according to the law of attraction, you will be blessed because of it. Plus, you'll have a cleaner closet in the process.

Now that you've cleared a path to see everything in your closet, it's time to redefine your identity. Build a whole new look around the existing pieces in your closet. Tap into your inner fashion designer. If you're the jeans and t-shirt type, rely on magazine layouts to help guide you. Or call that one friend who prides themselves on being a fashionista. Redo your look, your home, organize your office, and even give your car a good cleaning while you're at it. Moving simple pieces around in your home will make it feel like a brand-new place. With a new way of living and doing things, you'll feel empowered. Let's get started detoxing our closets, both in the literal and figurative sense.

Exercise #9 - CLOSET DECLUTTER

First, think of people you know who might be in need—a family who has fallen on hard times, a young person heading off to college who could use new clothing or other items, a friend who has always admired a lamp you never use because it sits in a living room that's never occupied, or an organization that supports those in need. Be of service to someone and let it go. Once you have the person in mind, write their name below in the left column. As we go through each room and begin our detoxing, we will write each item next to their name.

I know this may seem like more work than necessary. It would be easier to put the items in piles and tag them with a piece of paper. But the logging is for us, not for them. As we log, we will hopefully feel a few things: gratitude for the multitude of blessings we have, the spirit of giving, and the joy of putting a smile on someone else's face. We will also feel lighter and more ready to accept new blessings coming into our lives.

When we've completed our list, read it through one last time with the sole intention of speaking gratitude to the universe for blessing us with so much abundance. Thank the universe and expect to receive these blessings back tenfold. Setting intention is key.

NAME	ITEM	VALUE
Sister Tia	Barely warn black boots	$175.00
Will's 2nd Hand	Hi-back Black Leather Swivel Chair	$225.00
	TOTAL	**$400.00**

LET'S GO! And make sure to total all your items at the end. It's very important for your brain to see the monetary value so it's not referred to as trash. It's giving. It's abundance. (Feel free to use a blank sheet of paper if you need more space.)

NAME	ITEM	VALUE

NAME	ITEM	VALUE

DETOXING – FRIENDS & FAMILY

This can be another challenging area, especially when it comes to letting go of certain family members. Toxic people come in many forms and should not be given a free pass. AND yes, there's another "however" coming. However, remember the analogy: when you point a finger at someone, three fingers point back to you. This holds true for all people—not just those we like. That means when someone toxic shows up in your life, there's a lesson for YOU to learn. You are vibrating on a lower level. So it's important to clean up your vibration, and once you do, that person will either magically disappear or make an upward shift and join you on your higher vibrational level. Ultimately, this work is yours.

Take a day to reflect on all your friendships, family members, relationships, colleagues, and even foes. Narrow them down to those you've had an uncomfortable encounter with in the past two weeks. Write their names down in the space provided below. Then, follow the example and complete the exercise.

Being outspoken can sometimes make it difficult to hold your tongue in certain situations. However, mastering the art of quieting yourself, actively listening, and responding calmly but firmly when necessary can prove immensely beneficial. By standing your ground without engaging in drama, you can maintain clarity. Often, any negative tension between you and others will dissipate swiftly—either disappearing altogether or prompting you to gracefully disengage without harboring any lingering resentment. The beauty of handling situations this way is that if you see that person at an event, it would be easy to say hello, give them a hug, and keep moving. No animosity. You're no longer invested. The exercises below will guide you toward putting this into effect.

Exercise #10 - FRIENDS AND FAMILY

Step One: Recap the people and any situations that took place over the past week or two. You can choose to go as far back as you'd like, but make sure to focus on people currently in your life—whether from adulthood or your present school life, etc.

Sample Exercise: What I Take In

NAME	SITUATION
Diane	Constantly telling me how I am not a good friend, even after I just stopped what I was doing to help her handle something that had nothing to do with me.
Bee	Condescending, and snooty. She thinks she is better than me, and acts as if I don't know what I'm doing.

Samper Exercise: What I Put Out - Low Vibrational Behavior

NAME	SITUATION
Diane	I do not defend myself out of fear that I'll come across as rude. So, I wait until I explode, which ends up coming across as rude and defensive.
Bee	There's a part of me that feels I am not enough—not smart enough, and don't have the knowledge or skill set to contribute.

Samper Exercise: How I Replaced It.

NAME	REPLACEMENT
Diane	After having a conversation with her, I realized she would often belittle me, so when she took no accountability, I limited our interactions to texts and periodic phone calls.
Bee	I empowered myself and stopped playing small, so there was no need to care about what she thought of me.

WHAT I TAKE IN

NAME	REPLACEMENT

WHAT I PUT OUT

NAME	SITUATION

HOW I REPLACED IT

NAME	SITUATION

YOUR DETOXING SUMMARY

As you begin to truly embark on your life as the new you, you will start to feel empowered from the inside out. You might feel that this time it's real, and you're ready to stick to it and become the person you've just recreated. Even after committing to the new you, every now and then, the old tape will play to remind you, "I'm still here." Don't worry. You now have resources to stay ahead of those chemical surges; use your replacement tools to shift your energy from rowing upstream to an easy downstream flow. The more you practice, the more "it" becomes your new norm. Stay focused on the high-energy vibration. It's time for you to WIN!

"How can I accept 100% responsibility when I am not the only part of the equation?"

What difference does it make, really? Who owns what part? At the end of the day, do you want to be right, or do you want peace? All you should care about is what the other person showed up to teach you, so you can move on from it. Each party is 100% responsible for their participation. You have no control over what the other party decides to do—or not do. If they don't choose to learn and grow from their 100%, then so be it.

Once you accept 100% responsibility for your choices, take time to silently speak to each person or situation in the mirror. They were instrumental in you arriving at this new place. Thank them for serving as your teacher, your reflection, and tell them that without their help, you wouldn't have been able to see beyond what you believed to be true and shift the behavior. Tell them how much they are appreciated and how what they offered helped you immensely. Because of them, you are now able to move to your next level and live your life to its fullest.

As we close out, here are some of my quotes and affirmations that you can use when your "beautiful mind" wants to run amok. Tailor them to fit your life and journey if needed. It's up to you how many you would like to use. Space has been allotted for you to do so. Once you've selected the ones you want for yourself, pick one each day and live it out as if you've been cast in a leading role in a movie. If it's at night, set your intention before you go to bed; if it's in the morning, set your intention before leaving the house. Become one with it.

Exercise #11 - YOUR PERFECT LIFE

Choose one of the following affirmations to focus on as you prepare to start your day. This is NOT a writing exercise; it's about putting who you are into action. If it helps you to write the affirmation out first, that's fine. The key here is not just doing the exercise, but the energy you put into it. High vibrational energy will be essential for attracting what you want.

For example, if the affirmation I choose is, *"If it's true I teach people how to treat me, then I choose to treat myself like the queen that I am,"* here's how I will live it out:

Example - Living Your Day as the Queen or King You Are.

As you prepare to get dressed, select an outfit in your favorite color. Choose a hairstyle (if applicable) that matches your vibe. Maybe add a hat, shoes, handbag, or briefcase that feels empowering. As you step out the door, rain or shine, take control of your emotions and remind yourself that you are "the shit." When you encounter people, share a smile, say "good morning"—it doesn't matter if they acknowledge you back. This exercise is all about *you.*

When you arrive at your destination, bring that same energy inside with you. Be conscious of any person or situation that might offer a contrasting feeling. Stay ahead of it by setting your intention before you engage. You never know what someone else is going through or the vibration they're emitting, so it's important to proactively keep your energy high.

Perhaps a sweet treat could lift your mood or even someone else's—buy one for yourself or share it with others. You can't smile and frown at the same time. Maybe you can buy a cup of coffee for someone or have a cold drink waiting for the mail person. If there's someone at work who's shy or often ignored, ask them to join you for lunch.

Even if you're doing a task you don't enjoy, do it with joy. When confronted with rudeness or negativity, choose to keep joy in your heart and not let it steal your moment. Life is short, and it's not promised.

If your goal is to one day be the CEO of your own business, spend the day observing and learning. Take notes on how your current boss operates—pay attention to both the aspects you admire and those you don't. Notice your co-workers: Who works well with others? Who offers great customer service? This is your opportunity to gather insights and plot out the path that will lead you to your own success.

Choose one of the affirmations below. You can say it exactly as it's written, edit it to suit your needs, or find one that resonates more with you. Keep in mind, writing your own affirmation can be more personal, but might come with some resistance when executing the exercise. However, as long as you maintain positive, uplifting energy, the resistance will soon pass.

"YOU AFFIRM"

I am so thankful that today I woke up and everything else is profit!

_____

_____

_____

I don't have to know the HOW's of anything. Once I set what I want in place, I stand firm in knowing that the HOW's mean "**Help's On** *the* **W**ay!

_____

_____

_____

My direction may not always be clear, but I know that everything is happening for my highest good.

_____

_____

_____

Every cell and fiber in my body and of my being is functioning as GOD, in *Good Orderly Direction.*

_____

_____

_____

I attract everything I need because I **AM** everything I need and need to be.

_____

_____

_____

Because I am a magnet I set forth to attract only that which I believe to bring me joy, peace, health and prosperity.

_____

_____

_____

Like attracts like. If I want to know what I truly believe, think and feel I look at my life. If I don't like what you see, I become the change I want to see.

_____

_____

_____

Wherever I go, there I am. Who do I choose to take with me?

_____

_____

_____

It starts with me. When I show up to a place that doesn't feel good and everything and everyone around me is different, I guess it's safe to say I am the common denominator. I acknowledge and welcome the change.

_____

_____

_____

I will laugh my way to my new happy self.

_____

_____

_____

When creating a new me, I write out my character, dress her, give her a new walk and don't ever leave home without her.

_____

_____

_____

The Universe will align me with what I need when my purpose serves more than just my ego.

_____

_____

_____

When I continue to live in the past, I continue to halt my growth. When I choose to live in the present I have an opportunity to create the future I choose to have.

_____

_____

_____

Swans don't hang with Buzzards, so why should I? Reach above your norm.

_____

_____

_____

I teach others how to be their best self and reach for the stars by being my best self and reaching for my stars.

_____

_____

_____

I bring no value to a poor person's life by being a poor person myself.

_____

_____

_____

Forgiving has nothing to do with the person who has hurt me, it's all about me. I no longer choose to be held hostage by past situations.

_____

_____

_____

I choose to stand in my truth. For when I can't see the light, it must mean I have chosen to stand in the dark.

_____

_____

_____

If it's true I teach people how to treat me, then I choose to treat myself like the queen that I am.

_____

_____

_____

Blocks are blocks. I can continue to stumble on them or decide to step on, or go around them.

_____

_____

_____

Just because someone says it is so, doesn't make it so…, at least not when it refers to me.

_____

_____

_____

A choice is a choice, is a choice. I can choose happiness or I can choose unhappiness. My choice.

_____

_____

_____

Life sometimes brings me unhappy situations that I may have no choice over, but how long I choose to stay unhappy about it, well, that becomes my choice.

Even when I have no idea how to begin, if I am presented with an opportunity, it's a sign to begin.

Just because a person appears to know more than I do, don't make it so. Perhaps they are more confident in pretense but not qualified for the job.

When an idea comes through me, it's for me to do. Don't pass it off because I doubt myself.

I am never too old–Enough said!

_____

_____

_____

I am living today like tomorrow doesn't exist…, well technically it doesn't.

_____

_____

_____

Since I choose to continue to grow, I must accept I will most often be out of my comfort zone, but I choose to make my uncomfortable zone comforting.

_____

_____

_____

Because I am constantly creating my future, I pay attention to what I am doing at all times to ensure I am setting in motion a great place for myself to live in.

_____

_____

_____

It's easy to talk myself into whatever I want. So why not make it something GREAT!

When I feel rejected, I reselect my direction and… keep it movin'.

What do I like most about the script I created for my life?

The moment I decided no one was responsible for my happiness or success, I began to feel happy and live a successful life.

I have learned from everyone, and decided not to get mad when a person shows me what I truly believe and feel about myself.

I choose to be in love with myself, because there is no energy more powerful than the force of unconditional love.

My goal is to become what I want to share with others, to absorb every bit of it into my soul, and then pass it on to as many people as possible.

When people see my light, they are drawn to me and not even sure why.

Everyday, I step out in faith and walk in my purpose.

_____

_____

_____

I am grand and stand in my greatness. Shrinking and playing myself small does no one good.

_____

_____

_____

FINALE

Rewrite Your Life's Script

As we move into the "Finale," it's time to rewrite your script using the guide below. We'll write your script in the form of a treatment (blueprint) for your story. Don't limit your imagination. If you've always dreamed of living in a mansion, working from home, having a personal chef, driving a brand-new royal blue Mercedes convertible, sleeping until noon, and having the freedom to vacation anywhere in the world, this is your moment to write that script.

However, be mindful not to stretch so far that disbelief becomes the dominant energy. The energy we emit is key, so start from a believable place and gradually expand from there.

Steps to Writing Your Treatment

Your Title: The title is important. While your story can be fictional, try to keep at least some of your characters grounded in reality. This makes it easier to energetically align with your new life. Write out toxic, low-energy people quickly and focus on those who uplift you. The title should reflect the purpose of the story, which in this case is "Designing My Perfect Life." Before anyone reads your treatment, the title should give them a clear sense of what the story is about. Additionally, this title will serve as a reminder of your goals when you slip into old patterns. The moment you say the title, you'll have a clear vision of your story and your goal.

Write a Logline: Your log line will be an affirmation—one to three lines that capture the essence of your treatment. You can either choose an affirmation from the previous page or create your own. It should resonate with the tone and energy of your treatment.

Write Your Treatment: To begin, expand your logline into three acts: the beginning, middle, and end. Don't feel confined to writing them in order—if you know how you want the story to end, you might find it easier to start there and work backward. There are no hard rules—just your creativity guiding you.

Act One: The Setup
In Act One, introduce yourself and gradually introduce other characters and details about your life. By the end of this act, we should understand who you are, your personality, your lifestyle, and where the story is heading.

Act Two: The Confirmation
This act delves into the "meat and potatoes" of your daily life—what you set up in Act One. You might want to introduce a challenge or an old habit that you're working to overcome (this is optional). Perhaps your challenge could involve choosing between two exciting opportunities, like deciding between two job offers, selecting a car, or bidding on a new home. Regardless, the goal is to illustrate how your life looks in this new phase, with the added bonus of showing you navigating challenges in a healthier way.

Act Three: The Resolution
In this final act, resolve the challenges you've introduced in Act Two. Show how the old patterns or "old tape" arise, but this time, you handle them calmly and confidently. By the end of Act Three, we should have a clear understanding of who you are, what you do, how you live, and why.

Example of Act One:
This example on the following page will help get you started on the right track.

This Is The House That Terrah Built
Written by: Terrah Bennett Smith

LOGLINE/AFFIRMATION

"I'm living my life like it's golden. I have allowed the universe to bring me everything I've ever wanted, I have accepted it willingly, and it is right on time."

TREATMENT

This 5th Avenue tri-level penthouse apartment tells the story of my life. The first-floor living room is outfitted with exquisite furniture from the finest stores I discovered while traveling the world. The space is sparsely decorated, with a barely touched white baby grand piano that complements the mostly off-white décor. I've always dreamed of having an all-off-white room, and here it is. The air is filled with the scent of something delicious from my oversized gourmet kitchen. The buzz of the juicer is a morning ritual because my chef, a tall, handsome gentleman, knows that the first thing I want in the morning is the nutrients from a healthy drink. He collects a variety of organic vegetables from the juicer and pours them into a glass beside a plate of vegan breakfast choices.

As the chef makes his way through the house, he passes my quaint guest room—just large enough for a visitor but not for someone to move in—and my chic office, which is equipped with a sofa bed and television, just in case I fall asleep while working. The chef heads toward the stairs that lead to the lower level.

Upstairs, on the third floor, you'll find me, Terrah Bennett Smith—slender and put together, even in my comfy sweats or pajamas. My bedroom suite is perfectly laid out, occupying the entire third floor. It features a walk-in closet and a master bath suite, each the size of a typical living room. It's

5 AM on this beautiful Monday morning, and my internal alarm clock gently wakes me up. I glance at the clock and smile, then turn the TV channel to soundscapes. Closing my eyes, I begin my morning meditation. After 15-30 minutes, depending on the day ahead, I write in my gratitude journal, reflecting on what I am grateful for. Now, I am refreshed and ready to take on the day.

Downstairs, in the fitness room, which is below the main level, the chef has set up my food and drink. He places my green drink on the table next to my treadmill and sets my breakfast plate in a covered dish in the adjacent media room. This is where I continue my morning, listening to Abraham Hicks, Joe Dispenza, or another random life-changing coach. Across from the media room is the rehearsal studio—my space for working on projects, saving me the need to rent outside space.

I enter the fitness room, dressed and ready for my morning workout. I drink my green juice, hand the glass back to the chef with a "thank you," and begin my treadmill trot, feeling energized and focused for the day ahead.

The goal is for you and the reader to be able to visualize every color, outfit, and detail. You should hear everything—from the sound of the juicer to the aroma of the healthy meal being prepared. Keep writing until you've outlined at least a full day of your life as you envision it. I've provided space for your treatment with a guide, but feel free to create your own template if more space is needed. If you plan to make revisions over time, I recommend using a pencil or typing it on your computer.

Remember to title your script to reflect the essence of your story.

YOUR STORY

THINK BIG! HAVE FUN! CREATE!

Written by:

LOGLINE/AFFIRMATION

ACT ONE
(Treatment)

_____

_____

_____

_____

_____

_____

_____

_____

_____

_____

_____

_____

_____

_____

_____

_____

_____

_____

_____

_____

ACT TWO
(Treatment)

_____

_____

_____

_____

_____

_____

_____

_____

_____

_____

_____

_____

_____

_____

_____

_____

_____

_____

_____

_____

_____

_____

ACT THREE
(Treatment)

_____

_____

_____

_____

_____

_____

_____

_____

_____

_____

_____

_____

_____

_____

_____

_____

_____

_____

_____

_____

_____

THE END

Did you immerse yourself in the story as you were writing it?

Hopefully, you were able to see the picture clearly and feel the energy in every fiber of your being. You likely felt swept away in the fantasy of it, momentarily forgetting that you were simply writing it down. Do your best to hold onto that feeling and carry it with you every day.

Take a moment now to read the following affirmation aloud three times. As you do, maintain that intense energy and feel each word resonate deeply from within.

I have empowered my mind, granting it permission to think and attract beyond what I once believed to be possible. I have aligned with the universe to accept all the good that is set in motion for my behalf.

I have embedded positive visions and energy deep into my spirit, allowing the neurons of my brain, body, and soul to align with those things that are an energetic match.

I have stepped aside, and align with this effortless, unforced universe that which I desire. I remain open and unattached to any specific outcome, trusting that I will only be aligned with energies that match my truest desires and serve my highest good.

THOSE - OH REALLY, WO-O-O FEELINGS

I don't know about you, but the first time I decided to rewrite my script and dream BIG, it was hard to align with that energy. As I added the elements of my goals, I could feel myself doubting the possibility of this vision actually manifesting. *Oh really?* How do you plan to pull that off? Did any inner naysayers start to creep up?

When you try to align with something that feels out of your comfort zone, those "Oh really?" voices will make an appearance. If it's hard to align with your big vision, consider breaking it down into smaller steps. It's less daunting to start with something you can easily align with, rather than jumping straight from $5,000 in your bank account to manifesting a million dollars in one month. Begin with an amount that feels attainable, and as you gain confidence, gradually increase the goal until you're in alignment with your BIG vision.

Don't play it safe by sticking to what you know just because it feels comfortable. You do yourself—and this process—a disservice. The goal is to step into your grand self. Take it one step at a time, doing whatever feels good and has the least resistance. Remember: *Build it, and they will come.*

STOP NOW AND READ YOUR TREATMENT.

Read it with excitement and passion. If at any point you feel resistance to something you've written, stop and rewrite it. Keep adjusting it until it feels energetically aligned with your vision. Your treatment should be easy and believable, not forced.

Practice! Practice! Practice!

For those of you who reached for the stars and are flowing with ease—congratulations!

Remember, life's contrasts are inevitable. No amount of vision boards, affirmations, positive sticky notes, chanting, fasting, or prayer will shield you from their arrival. These contrasts are necessary for growth. So instead of fighting them (which creates an upstream energy), embrace them. Use your tools to move through them effortlessly and with grace.

Exercise #12 - CANCEL THAT!

ACT #	WHAT?	WHY?	WHEN?	NOW WHAT?
1	Penthouse apt. on 5th avenue	Too expensive I have never believed I'd be able to afford something like that.	I'm too old now, and everyone I know who have wanted something similar has achieved it long before my age.	I choose to focus on the steps I have made to achieve that penthouse apartment. This book, speaking engagements, talks shows, etc.

You Can Have at it.

ACT #	WHAT?	WHY?	WHEN?	NOW WHAT?

NOW WHAT?

Continue to do the work, and one day, you'll look up and realize you've arrived at your destination. Let go of the pressure of having a specific time frame to get everything done. The journey is what you will remember the most. Once you reach the destination, you'll be contemplating where to go next.

There's something about reaching the third trimester of your life that makes you question whether you've truly lived up to your full potential. That realization can push you into gear. For me, I had to take control of *me*. I had to say no to people who kept hurting my feelings, and I had to silence my mind when it wanted to revert to what was familiar—without any real reason to do so. I had to get back to seeing my life as I had once envisioned it: my beautiful penthouse, townhome, or whatever my highest good had in store for me.

Rewriting my script—this book and the accompanying short film—is my way of sharing my grand self with the world. Everything I've done over the years has been packaged into this 5-B's project. What started as me simply directing and writing the short film soon evolved. Out of nowhere, I received a divine message to rewrite it and cast myself as an actress. Now, everything I've specialized in—acting, writing, directing, producing—is all part of one sweet package, ready to serve many people.

For years, I created projects for myself, only to give the role I wrote for me to a friend to help them out. My excuse was always that I was directing and just wanted to focus on that. *Bullshit!* I've been directing for years. Some of my friends who started directing recently did so with the intent to put themselves in their own projects. If they can do it, why couldn't I? I was playing small, limiting myself. How could I ask to be blessed with acting roles if I wasn't willing to honor myself? Enough of that! I am proud to be a jack-of-all-trades: acting, singing, directing, writing, producing, managing, mothering, empowering—and mastering all of them.

What about you? Is there something you've always wanted to try but felt it was too late, or you were too old? Do you think you don't have enough money or aren't the "right type" for the job? What have you learned about yourself while doing the exercises in Acts 1-3? Are you still feeling doubtful? That's okay. We've all lived long enough to know that breaking patterns is hard. Depending on how old you are and how long you've dealt with a certain block, it could take years. After all, it took years for that block to form.

STAND IN YOUR POWER!

Now the excitement begins. I've done years of work, and finally, I feel aligned with my highest good. I'm on a mission to stay on track and not let old habits resurface to get in my way. It's time to let my inner light shine.

When I was in my twenties, a random psychic told me I would be known for my work globally—but not until my fifties or sixties. That wasn't the timeline I was hoping for. I had already spent decades pursuing my dreams. Another thirty-ish years? It felt like an eternity. I was focused on the end result, unaware that those years would be filled with life experiences that were necessary for the new person I was becoming.

I often ask myself, *Why now?* Why didn't I have the drive and fortitude to stay aligned ten years ago? I now understand that the level of commitment it takes to stay the course is a lifelong journey. It doesn't go away; it just gets easier to manage. It becomes second nature—and that takes time to master. Now that I'm an empty-nester, I have more time to invest in myself, all day long if I choose. Because I'm willing and ready to enjoy this phase of my life, I am standing in my power, owning it, and being unapologetically selfish. Why not do the same for yourself?

As I mentioned earlier in the book, I started writing in 2012, and now, in 2025, I'm finishing it. I could spend time kicking myself for how long it took, but the truth is, *now* is the right time. Who I've become, what I've learned, and how I've grown—this book is birthing at the perfect time.

I had to be explicit about what I wanted to accomplish and give those goals deadlines. I never got upset if the deadlines needed to shift; I just made sure they didn't get pushed away indefinitely. Life happens while we make plans, so it's fine to make adjustments. Just be aware that your reason for shifting a deadline isn't due to a lack of commitment—or worse, fear.

Exercise: 13 - Goals

GOAL	DETAILS & DESCRIPTION *(TERRAH FIX DATES)*
Finish My Book	Complete the first draft of my book by May 31, 2024. Finish rough draft read through by June 9th. Give it to the editor by June 10th. Editor's draft to be completed by June 24th. Between June 10-24th I will research online self-publications. June 24th do a final read though completed by June 29th. June 29th upload it to an online publication.
Acting	Star in or co-star in a feature film, whether my own project or cast in a project.
Speaking	Set up at least one speaking engagement and screening of my film and accompanying book

In this next exercise, you will log what you plan to accomplish within the next six months. Be very specific. Don't let money or accessibility limit your vision. However, before you write anything down, make sure these goals align with the work you've been doing throughout this book. There should be no doubt in your mind that you can manifest these goals. The key here is to create from a place of unwavering belief.

If you experience even a hint of doubt while logging your goals, DO NOT add that goal to your log at this time. Instead, focus on replacing the doubt with affirmations, and when you are absolutely certain you have the belief and commitment to see it through to fruition, then you can write it down. This log is for the things you KNOW WILL and MUST happen for you.

Also, remain open to "THIS OR SOMETHING BETTER." Remember, we are setting our intentions for what we want, but we must leave space for the universe to deliver the best possible outcomes for us. It would be amazing to tell someone, "I always wanted to be on a hit television show, but I had no idea I would create it, star in it, and even go on to direct several episodes." That is "THIS OR SOMETHING BETTER."

GOAL	DETAILS & DESCRIPTION

You Are Never Too Old

There is no time frame or limit for when you can start over or should have reached your goal. As long as you have breath, you CAN—and owe it to yourself—to go after what you want. If you found out you only had a year left to live, wouldn't you want to live it with zest, doing and being everything you've dreamed of? No excuses. Just be it.

Keep Your Vibrational Energy High

This goes hand in hand with acknowledging and replacing. To stay focused on the direction you want to go, you must speak, feel, and vibrate in that direction. Remember, you attract what you give energy to.

Paying Attention Is Key

To connect the dots in your life and avoid repeating the same patterns, you must pay attention. If journaling or keeping a daily log helps, don't dismiss what's happening as mere happenstance. Everything has meaning.

Wherever You Go, There You Are

When situations repeat themselves and all the elements—people, places—change, but you remain the common denominator, it's time for self-reflection. People often serve as mirrors for us. Don't be too quick to blame others; chances are, it's something within you. Thank them for showing you what you need to work on, then do the work. Watch how the situation and the people begin to shift.

Change Starts With You—From Within

Detoxing your food, your closet, your mental state, and more goes hand in hand with becoming the "new you." Imagine reaching your goal only to discover a health issue from poor diet, or that you're 50 pounds overweight due to lack of exercise because you were too mentally consumed by life's mishaps. You're out of alignment with the energy you wish to attract. Get aligned.

Acknowledge And Replace

Simply saying, "I will no longer think or do this," is not enough. Habits are hard to break, especially when they've been a part of your life for a long time, often forming a chemical relationship with them. Even if it seems they've disappeared for weeks, they can resurface. Unless you replace them with what you want to manifest, you'll continue to ride the emotional rollercoaster of those lower vibrational behaviors. Contrast is real and necessary.

See Yourself as Grand

Everyone wants to aspire to something or feel good about themselves. Not many people aspire to live in illness or poverty. The better you are at living in your greatness, the more people you can serve. If you need to fake it until you make it, go for it. By doing it and believing it long enough, you'll eventually become it. There's nothing wrong with being grand. Swans don't hang out with buzzards

ENCORE

YOUR PERFECT LIFE - DAILY ROUTINE

When You Wake Up:

- Before starting your day, take time to align yourself.
- Meditate/Prayer
- Write down what you're grateful for.
- Stretch! It doesn't have to be an extensive gym workout. Not everyone has the time or desire for that. Find a 10-minute stretch, full-body workout, or yoga session on YouTube. There are plenty of options, from yoga and Pilates to ab work and full-body toning. No excuses!

Plan Your Perfect Life:

- Dress the part. Choose an outfit that aligns with the character you've described in your treatment. Pay attention to your hair, makeup, accessories, and shoes. You don't need to spend a fortune to pull it off. Remember, you are now the STAR of your own production—act like it!
- Make healthy eating choices for all meals.

Live Out Your Perfect Life Every Day:

- Stay ahead of contrasting energy. It might come from a person on the bus or a car that cuts you off. You and only you can choose how to respond. So, take a deep breath and choose to maintain a higher vibration.

- Walk and carry yourself as if you are already living your best life.
- Do your best to stay on a higher vibration throughout the day.
- Perform periodic alignment exercises. Turn inward, repeat a few affirmations, and express gratitude. It's always beneficial.
- Keep your music, television, and other forms of entertainment positive. Avoid the news, combative reality shows, and mindless scrolling through social media. The effects may be subtle, but over time, you align with what you consume—good or bad.

When You Arrive Home:

- Recap your day and reflect on how it went.
- Set your intentions for how you want tomorrow to unfold.
- Late-night meditation is a great way to wind down.
- Say a few words of gratitude, then go to bed.

www.ingramcontent.com/pod-product-compliance
Lightning Source LLC
Chambersburg PA
CBHW051205120626
46547CB00013B/1211